A NEW APPROACH TO DISCIPLINE:

LOGICAL CONSEQUENCES

A NEW APPROACH TO DISCIPLINE:

LOGICAL CONSEQUENCES

by

RUDOLF DREIKURS, M.D.
AND
LOREN GREY, Ph.D.

HAWTHORN BOOKS
A division of Elsevier-Dutton
New York

Library of Congress Catalog Card Number: 68-28720

ISBN: 0-8015-4632-X

10

Preface

For the past fifteen years we have devoted the major share of our time to the dissemination of knowledge about the behavior of children—their motivations and the means by which they can be redirected. We have followed the lead of Alfred Adler who as a psychiatrist—like the senior author —was concerned greatly with the problems of raising children and educating them. He also saw, as we do, that an understanding of how to bring up children in this troubled age is vitally needed by both parents and teachers if we are to correct the mistakes of the past. Most of the books by the senior author have been devoted to either parent or teacher education as separate functions. Combining the work of psychiatry and teacher education, we attempt to present and explain essential principles about child behavior which we feel can be equally useful at home or in the classroom.

How to deal with children and youth has become a major problem in our time. The war between the generations is taking on increasingly ominous proportions. We, as parents and teachers, must concentrate our efforts on enabling ourselves to deal effectively with our young people, who are demanding equal participation in our society, often in ways which we feel are threatening its values. This effort will require a profound reconstruction of our methods and premises. We need to recapture the ability to influence our children, an ability which we lost because few of us, as adults, could turn our autocratic role of a boss into the democratic leadership of a guide.

It is not easy to give up old cherished ideas and procedures. The critical condition of the field of education makes this mandatory. We sincerely hope that this book will present some challenging ideas which may provide the stimulation for a necessary reorientation of parents and teachers.

We wish to acknowledge our appreciation to Mr. William Monson for his editorial assistance in the preparation of this book.

R. D.
L. G.

Contents

A NEW APPROACH TO DISCIPLINE: LOGICAL CONSEQUENCES

PART I

Theoretical Considerations

CHAPTER 1

Why Is a New Tradition Needed?

In Southampton, Long Island, a group of 127 young socialites gathered in a mansion for one of the season's most elaborate debutante parties. During the night they went on a rampage, ripping down chandeliers, breaking windows, and destroying furniture. Their explanation: They had none.

In East Los Angeles, a carload of young hoodlums attacked a high school teacher and several students when asked to move their car, which was blocking the exit of a parking lot. Their reason: They didn't like being told what to do.

In a midwestern city, a group of teen-agers threw out a system of power lines, plunging the city into darkness. Their alibi: They were "bored" and didn't know what to do about it.

In New York, Oakland, Los Angeles, and other cities, high-school youths terrorize the halls, attacking teachers and other students. Their reason: "prejudice."

On high school and college campuses across the country, students picket, march, and demonstrate. Their "causes" vary, but always the tenor is the same: discontent, anger, protest.

The FBI notes that juvenile delinquency is rising at a

much more rapid rate than the growth of the population. Worried police officials point to an even more alarming statistic: Attacks on police officers are mounting, and co-operation with all branches of law enforcement are decreasing.

The slick-magazine writers are kept busy explaining how all this came to be; and "Dear Abby" devotes as much space to parent-child problems as to advice to the lovelorn.

It is our thesis that the whole modern adolescent generation is at war with adults and not just an extremist group of delinquents. However, it is becoming apparent that the age at which our young people are turning to delinquency is *decreasing*. We are also becoming aware of perhaps another even more distressing phenomenon—that these acts of violence and destruction are not confined to those children ordinarily considered as coming from "across the tracks" but are being manifested among all social and economic segments of our society. At this point, no home in America can be considered exempt. No parent today can safely feel that none of his children might become one of these vandals.

We are becoming aware that the attitudes of today's children, regardless of age, are quite different from what they were in "the good old days." Children no longer accept parents' judgments as absolute. Indeed, in many cases they pay little or no attention to them at all. Parents are called upon to justify their actions in ways which were not expected of them in the past. In addition, defiance and even outright rebellion are becoming more characteristic of even very small children. Fifty, or even thirty years ago, no child would dream of "getting the law" on his parents after he had been beaten by his father. Today this is a relatively commonplace occurrence. In more than one instance we have read where children have shot and killed their parents for some real or fancied grievance that they might hold. Far more frequent are the covert or hidden manifestations of this rebellion, the *unwillingness* rather than the inability of children to learn, to function, and to cooperate in the school and at home.

As has been mentioned, of course, the extreme manifestation of this is in the behavior of our teen-agers. Though generally unrecognized as yet by the community at large, the growing acts of juvenile delinquency represent little less than outright warfare between these delinquents and society. It has been suggested that the basis for this warfare is far more profound than has been previously assumed, and that, in reality, the entire adolescent generation is involved. Perhaps even more than this, adolescents resent the unwillingness of the adult community to give them any part in deciding about activities and regulations regarding their own welfare. Perhaps the only hopeful sign in the picture at present is that more and more young people are joining the constructive movements which are working to shape our country's future. The Peace Corps and some of the groups attempting to achieve racial equality in this country are perhaps the best examples of this. At least some young people are finding fulfillment in the kind of creative and cooperative activity which is the best counteraction for the poisons which have led to the war between the generations.

At the same time, however, another movement is also growing at an alarmingly rapid rate and recruiting many of our young people in its ranks. Though often young people may be able to channel their hostilities and desires to rebel against authority in a relatively constructive direction, such as in some of the racial equality movements, all too often they are taken in by the openly hostile delinquent groups and thus further directed away from achieving status in the community. There are those who contend that today's rebels are an inevitable by-product of the democratic process; but their number and activities are increasing at a rate that leaves us little room for complacency. The attitude of throwing up one's hands is also becoming more prevalent in this area, as well as in adult-child relationships, when we attempt to deal with the problem.

UNDERLYING SOURCES OF THE PROBLEM

Numerous theories have been advanced to attempt to explain some of the facts that have been presented. One psychoanalytic writer, in commenting on the vandalism committed by the young socialites at the Long Island party, called the act the result of "mass psychosis." He suggested that their underlying need was "to be punished," because they felt that their parents had not been firm enough with them as young children. Another writer has suggested that these children suffer from what he calls "anomic"—the feeling of rootlessness, of being cut off or not belonging to other members of society. Still others have suggested that in this materialistic age children are suffering from what is called decay in moral and spiritual values. Perhaps there is an element of truth in all of these statements, but they appear to suffer from the shortcomings that characterize most theories of this sort. Either the theorists are attempting to treat only symptoms, or their concepts are so vague and general as to have little specific bearing on the situation confronting us. They appear also to have little understanding of the forces and events which are shaping the world of to-day and tommorrow.

The factor which would seem to underlie the whole scope of these problems is the rapid and overwhelming social upheaval which is taking place in our current era. The first of such changes occurred some eight to ten thousand years ago when primitive men started to break down the tribal chains and establish the beginnings of modern civilization.

Primitive society, which was relatively homogenous, gave way to the caste and class system of civilization.

The early myths and tales of all civilized peoples include stories of man in revolt—against his gods, his rulers, his competitors. Adam, Cain, and Prometheus, all rebelled—and suffered accordingly. So did Brunhilde, Medea, and Antigone, on the feminine side.

Thus, civilization has been a constant revolt of one group displacing its former rulers and leading to a new order and a new rebellion. The world has been a long time "going to the dogs." Why is the current trend more acute and more dangerous?

Today, with the advent of democracy, the previously suppressed can openly rebel; women, the colored races, labor, the poor, and children rebel openly against authoritarian domination. In a democracy, each individual can no longer be denied or deprived of his dignity and value. Man no longer is willing to be an insignificant particle of a mass.

Old-style authoritarianism still exists. Two fifths of the world's people still live under some sort of dictatorship. But resistance is building up to the old and the new forms of domination, and that resistance follows similar tactics, wherever the suppressed, neglected, or disrespected claim their equal right and value.

There is a similar desire behind all forms of revolts: to be recognized as an equal. This is what Alfred Adler formulated as possibly the first social law—the law of equality, the ironclad logic of social living which demands recognition of every human being as an equal.[1]

Though this trend is prevalent in all countries, it is in the United States—perhaps also in Israel—that the manifestations of a desire for equality overshadow all aspects of political and community activities. As a result of our affluence, those who do not share in it press hardest for their share. From the beginning, equality has been a continuing theme in the story of the United States. It received prominent mention in all our founding documents. Lincoln called it "The father of all moral principle, . . . the electric cord in that Declaration that links the hearts of patriotic and liberty loving men together, . . . a hope to the world for all future kind." [2] De Tocqueville [3] considered the equality principle the outstanding aspect of the American states. Thus it is that the United States has become the archetype of the revolution of the striving for equality. Despite this preoccupation with equality, its very nature is seldom comprehended. We replaced the principle of equal opportunity for the recognition of equal rights and even more for the realization of equal human worth. While we have more actual social and political equality, we do not know how to live with each other as equals.

The strife for equality affects not only individuals, but all

---

[1] Alfred Adler, *Social Interest: A Challenge to Mankind*, London, Faber & Faber, 1938.

[2] *Abraham Lincoln: Selected Speeches, Messages and Letters*, New York, Holt, Rinehart and Winston, 1964.

[3] Alexis de Tocqueville, *Democracy in America*, London, Oxford University Press, 1952 (first published in 1835).

groups as well, races, creeds, professions and labor, sexes—
and most recently, age groups. Presently, the struggle for
equality is most strongly focused on color; the Freedom
movement concerns itself mostly with the rights of Negroes
and their disadvantages, in contrast to the white population.
The struggle for equal status of members of different reli-
gions is almost over. The right of labor is still contested but
concealed by the concern with specific issues to be settled.
As far as the war between the sexes is concerned, a tenuous
truce exists. Women, in their effort to gain equal status and
treatment as men, often manage to find themselves in the
favored position, sometimes replacing the traditional inferior role with one of moral and cultural superiority. As the
desire of Negroes to be equal leads them to the concept of
black power, so women, in order to avoid humiliating inferiority, often act as the superior sex. In all these areas, the
fight for equality is well recognized; but few begin to see
that it has greatly affected the relationship between children
and adults. Children refuse to be treated as inferior; they
rebel against domination and become tyrants.

One point should be noted: Though there are equality
campaigns on many fronts, none of them has been won.
Thus, all of them are currently in action, and their struggles
overlap to the point of obscuring that fact. An excellent example of several revolts wrapped up in one might be this:
a teen-age Negro girl dressed as a beatnik and reading a
copy of *The Feminine Mystique* while engaged in a sit-in
for a grape-picker's strike. This girl herself might not be
able to decide just which of her causes—Negro, youth,
woman, labor—most moves her at that given moment, but
she is driven by them all. The wise observer will note that

she represents a striving for equality in each and is thus more powerfully driven by their combined impetus.

The war between the generations is as old as the war between the sexes. Wherever one group sets itself up as a dominant power, it violates the logic of social living and creates rebellion. The rebellion of women and of children is evident throughout our civilization. However, it never could break into the open because society supported the dominant group, that is, men and adults. Today this rebellion is no longer concealed but open. Only few are aware of the fact that the difficulties which we have with our children are a result of the war between the generations. Kvaraceus [4] recognizes the universal nonconformity of children. He speaks about the "continuum of norm-violating behavior." On the one end of the continuum are the children whom you can't get up in the morning, or to bed in the evening, who fight with their brothers and sisters, refuse to put their things away, or to do their homework or to help around the house, who either eat too much or too little, do too much or too little—in other words, the average American child. And on the other extreme of the continuum is the juvenile delinquent with his open defiance of society and its norms. There is no qualitative, only a quantative difference between them. The delinquent is more outspoken in violence in his rebellion. However, Kvaraceus does not see this nonconformity as a fight for children's rights, but as an intrusion of low-class morality into middle- and upper-class society. It was the German educator Wyneken [5] who emphasized the

[4] W. C. Kvaraceus and others, *Delinquent Behavior*, Washington, D.C., National Education Association, 1959.
[5] Gustav Wyneken, *Schule und Jugend Kultur*, Jena, Dietrichs, 1919.

rights of youth and its self-determination. And Montessori,[6] shortly before her death, published a touching appeal for disarmament in education, calling for an end of the warfare which exists in our homes and schools. There appears little question that children today have much more *freedom* than they did in the past; but freedom is not equality. Because children feel they are denied genuine participation in the community, they refuse to accept the responsibilities that go with freedom. At the same time they demand more and more rights. Today's children feel that they have little to say in the decisions that affect their welfare; accordingly, they turn to the pursuit of pleasure as a means of compensating for this neglect. On the other hand, adults do not want to give up their control even though in many respects this control is an illusion. We expect our children to conform to the values which we thrust upon them, and do not understand why they refuse to accede to our demands.

In reality, the problem is much deeper. In any culture where values are subjected to sudden and dramatic change, the transition period during which the old values are cast off and new ones assumed is inevitably painful. We are experiencing the consequences of this newly found freedom and we are yet unable to deal with it adequately. We vacillate between giving in to children's demands because it seems easier and we love them, and to using the outmoded authoritarian methods of old in attempts to correct the mistakes that they inevitably make.

[6] Maria Montessori, "Disarmament in Education," *The Montessori Magazine*, Vol. 4, 1950.

HISTORICAL TRENDS AND OUR ATTITUDES
TOWARD CHILDREN

It will be helpful here to undertake a review of how our attitudes toward children have changed and how these developments have influenced the ways in which we deal with them today.

One of the most significant beliefs in many Western cultures is the notion of original sin. While we do not intend to argue the merits of it as theology, we must acknowledge it held sway for hundreds of years and still underlies many of the methods parents use in dealing with children. Stated simply, original sin was Adam's rebellion against God's orders. This sin, which Adam committed in the Garden of Eden, has been, by God's edict, handed down from generation to generation. Man is thus born guilty of sin (or ironically, in light of our theme, of *rebellion*). Some of this guilt, however, can be mitigated by learning to live virtuous lives or gaining salvation through faith.

The stigma of this guilt at birth was great. In the most extreme forms of religious practice, children were severely, often brutally, dealt with in the name of virtue. Play was considered frivolous, work and study hours were deliberately designed to be long, hard, and painful. The political and economic attitudes of the time were attuned with these ideas and resulted in most children being treated only a little better than slaves. At the same time, since the Middle Ages, these ideas were fully consonant with the prevailing concepts which allowed freedom for only those associated with royalty or with the clergy.

The process of education, as could be easily seen, followed very much along the same lines. Formal schooling was reserved only for the clergy and the members of the ruling classes. Notions about learning held that the mind was a muscle and therefore could be trained only by long painful hours of drill and exercise. Consequently, the lot of children in those days, whether educated or not, was obviously not a very happy one. Families were, for the most part, large, and children found little opportunity to assume a special position and were forced to accept the subordinate roles assigned to them.

Perhaps the first major voice to question the validity of the prevailing ways of treating children was that of Rousseau, when he published his controversial *Émile* in 1762.[7] He particularly took issue with the concept of original sin and asserted that the harshness and rigidity with which children were treated merely tended to brutalize them rather than allow them to develop as decent human beings. In his view the education of the day was much more of a handicap than an asset. Rousseau also felt that education should be adapted to the needs of the learner and should not interfere with his normal development. Childhood should be a happy rather than a grim time; play should be encouraged, not condemned as sinful, and the words "obey" and "command" should be banished from the child's vocabulary. Each child should receive education up until the age of twelve; rather than to attempt to inculcate virtue and truth, teachers and parents should attempt merely to exclude vice and error. The child must learn to do right, not as something that ought to be done to obey adult orders, but only to escape the painful consequences of wrong action. Here

[7] J. J. Rousseau, *Émile,* selections ed. by William Boyd, New York, Bureau of Publications, Teachers College, Columbia University, 1962.

we can see the beginnings of the concept of natural consequences which was to be expounded by Herbert Spencer a hundred years later, and yet remained virtually neglected until the present day.

In many other areas of thought Rousseau was more conventional, if not reactionary. He started what has become an endless controversy. Its ultimate influence has been prodigious. William T. Harris, one of Rousseau's most ardent and constant critics, was prompted to suggest that without *Émile* there could be no understanding of Pestalozzi, Froebel, or for that matter, of any great educator of the twentieth century.[8]

However, despite the philosophic upheaval his ideas provoked, Rousseau had very little effect on the customs and manners of his own time. Herbert Spencer,[9] writing a hundred years later, still found it necessary to call attention to the excessive harshness with which the parents of his era disciplined children. Spencer, Herbart, Froebel, and later Maria Montessori, now revered as pioneers in attempts to alter the prevailing concepts about children, also had very little influence on educational practices of their day.

It remained for three men at the turn of the last century to create the foundation for the revolution in child-rearing practices and educational methods which was to sweep the world. Binet of France discovered that children even in the lowest socioeconomic groups had intelligence equal to those in the wealthy classes. In Vienna, Freud completed the basic framework for his theory of psychoanalysis. John

8 William T. Harris, preface to *Émile*, ed. Boyd, *op. cit.*, p. 1.
9 Herbert Spencer, *Essays on Education and Kindred Subjects*, ed. Charles W. Eliot, New York, E. P. Dutton & Co., 1963.

Dewey,[10] writing in America, laid the groundwork for the concepts of progressive education.

It is difficult to assess whose influence among the three was most important in bringing about the change in our attitudes regarding the child. Binet furnished us with the tools by which we learned that intelligence does not depend on class, race, or economic status. Freud and his followers literally frightened parents and teachers out of some of the barbaric and inhuman practices of suppressing the child, particularly of the excessive use of physical punishment and moralizing which was characteristic of adults of the earlier generations. However, the influence of John Dewey would seem to have been more profound—at least in America. He brought us much closer to the idea of true equality in education than we had ever experienced before.

Dewey believed that schooling should be for all children, not for the privileged few. Under his influence the focus of educational practice was shifted from emphasis on purely vocational or intellectual pursuits to consideration of the social and emotional needs of the child. He pointed out that all too often subject matter was being taught as an end in itself rather than a means by which we can more effectively function as mature human beings. Perhaps even more important, he revived Rousseau's idea that self-determination rather than submission to so-called higher authority should be the basis on which we act. Creativity, spontaneity, self-decision were to him the basic characteristics which should influence the development of the child.

The fact that progressive education, as envisioned by Dewey as a method of teaching, was never totally adopted

[10] John Dewey, *Democracy and Education*, New York, The Macmillan Co., 1914.

in its pure form in most schools in the United States does not alter the profound influence that his ideas have had upon our way of life.

Two problems ultimately contributed to a drastic inhibition of the effectiveness of progressive teaching methods. A vastly greater amount of teaching skill than heretofore was needed in order to successfully apply them.

One of the major consequences of this was often an abdication of teacher leadership which led to a kind of permissive anarchy that made learning—not to mention maintenance of discipline, or even the promotion of democratic principles themselves—nearly impossible. These were perhaps the most important reasons why this concept in its pure form really never gained a total hold on education in America. At the same time it can be said that John Dewey's ideas expanded the concept of educational equality in America to the point where it is now a constitutional guarantee, and considered inherent in the very nature of democracy.

Another very powerful influence on American attitudes about children emerged from the teachings of Freud. This influence, though helping in many ways to weaken the authoritarian views held about children prior to this time, unfortunately strengthened the leaderless "laissez-faire" type of permissiveness just mentioned. This concept flourished in American classrooms and homes, particularly in the middle thirties. Its basis was that the humiliation, belittling, and oppressive moralizing characteristic of teachers and parents in earlier years had not stimulated children to try harder. It had instead increased their feeling of guilt and repressed hostility which emerged in more subtle, but sometimes more dangerous, forms. There is no doubt that adherence to these doctrines produced a radical change in parent and teacher behavior during this time.

In the thirties we witnessed a theory of freedom for the child to develop at his own pace with his own resources, which had been advocated by Rousseau two hundred years before. Unfortunately, in their zeal to protect the ego of the child from damaging adult punishments, the followers of Freud neglected or unintentionally underemphasized one essential fact: With freedom comes responsibility. The result was chaos. Children literally became the masters of the adults. Parents were afraid to stand up to their offspring for fear that even the assertion of parental rights would be experienced as humiliation and rejection and would arouse dangerous guilt feelings in the child. Frustrated teachers were in effect told that even the rights of others in the group were less important than satisfying the "needs" of the individual child. Freudian concepts and John Dewey's views on progressive education may have freed the child from centuries of brutality and oppression; but they failed to provide the means by which he could properly function in such an atmosphere of freedom.

Adler had tried to meet this challenge; but his ideas were first overshadowed by the more titillating theories of Freud, and then neglected when opposition arose to the excesses and errors of Freudian educational psychology. His theory of psychology, coupled with Dewey's theories of democratic education, might have produced a truly revolutionary and practical educational system in America. Unfortunately, both Dewey and Adler have been stigmatized by their rejection of Freudian psychology, and the great experiment has never been attempted until now. Only recently have the positive results obtained through the application of Adlerian principles become recognized in the States. The principles now are gaining steadily in influence and momentum.

Adler [11] rejected autocratic methods of dealing with children, but he opposed also the extreme indulgence suggested by Freud's followers, based on the assumption that all the child needs is love. The constant emphasis on the child's needs for love and acceptance led to an unprecedented degree of indulgence and submission to the child's demands. For Adler, the essential theme was cooperation rather than permissiveness; but he emphasized that cooperation could not take place without the acceptance of responsibility. Though Adler agreed that humiliation was extremely harmful to the child, he also recognized that indulgence could be even worse. Mutual respect and shared responsibility was recognized as the basis for democratic living. Life thus was not a seesaw struggle between the demands of the individual and the welfare of the group. The question was not how permissive or how strict one should be; what was needed was a willingness to understand the child and to stimulate his cooperation. Restraints on children were necessary; but they were always to be arranged wth the view to teaching the child what he could do for and with his fellowman.

THE RETURN TO AUTHORITARIANISM

Disillusioned with ultrapermissiveness and increasingly frustrated in their inability to deal effectively with their children, adults have swung once more toward authoritarian methods in their dealings with children. The paddle has

[11] Alfred Adler, *The Education of Children*, London, Allen & Unwin, 1957.

been reintroduced into the school program. The prevailing cry is for more homework, a return to the three R's, and the teaching of subjects as subjects rather than as tools for the attainment of skills with which to function in our complex society.

To excuse the failure of our educational practices, a villain had to be found. The scapegoat chosen was a concept which did not exist in reality; nonetheless, it could be a convenient whipping boy for anyone who chose to use it. This was "progressive education."

It does not exist today, and even in the mid-thirties heyday of Dewey and Freud it had little general acceptance. Opposition to its excesses effectively did away with it two decades ago; yet recently we have witnessed extraordinary efforts being made against its image. Behind these efforts seems to be a much greater fear than that of falling behind the Communists or of weakening our nation through permissive, sloppy education. This is the apprehension that has invaded almost every segment of our present-day life—the fear of *too much freedom*. Thus, because in the thirties progressive education became associated in the public consciousness with the concepts of permissive freedom and liberal ideas, its poor cadaver has been exhumed today to serve as a straw man for those who fear the growth of too much freedom.

We Americans seem unable to deal yet with the kind and amount of liberty that today's women, children, Negroes, and labor unions are attaining. We are looking to the authoritarian methods of the past as a means to resolve our tension over this issue. The extremist movements in politics, in education, in parent-child training have their roots in this same fear. The hate we see growing all around us is the result. In reality, there is no ill of democracy which cannot be cured by more democracy.

We can perhaps now see why the rebellion of our teen-agers is becoming more intense. Children are unwilling to accept these new restrictions and oppressions forced upon them by adults. The rebellion may take only the form of failure to learn under a guise of inability, or it may take some of the more violent forms which we chronicled earlier. Either way, the situation is critical.

"Freedom" and "liberty" were once cherished words in the United States; today they are words tainted by fear. To-morrow they might well be ones of hate. It could happen; Huxley and Orwell gave us a picture of that tomorrow. We are learning day by day how that picture comes to be.

It is for these reasons that a new tradition in child-rear-ing is so desperately needed. The traditional methods of rais-ing children are obsolete; they do not bring the desired re-sult in a democratic setting. Essentially, the aim of this new tradition is to help the parent and the teacher to learn to cope with today's children on the basis of equality and mu-tual respect. Parents need help to understand children so that they may be able to help them to live in freedom and with shared responsibility. Through this understanding of children, adults may find it easier themselves to live as equals in our democratic era.

For their part, the children will learn that unless they accept the responsibilities that go with their new freedom, they only create another form of authoritarianism—one which could become even more savage and oppressive than that of the past. The keystone of our theory is the belief that children cannot be taught to take on responsibility unless it is given to them. Today children are free to do as they please and the adults have to take on the responsibility of their acts.

The hoped-for result of the application and practice of a new relationship as proposed here will be a world where everyone, regardless of race or sex or age, lives together in a society of freedom with responsibility, of democratic cooperation, with each contributing according to his ability and receiving the benefits of his efforts accordingly without prejudice, without punishment.

CHAPTER 2

The Development of Personality

In order to understand more thoroughly the rationale behind the proposed application of new approaches, it is necessary to make certain assumptions about the nature of man. These assumptions are derived in whole or part from the theories of Alfred Adler as amplified and elaborated in earlier writings.[1] In view of the controversies surrounding most psychological theories today and the deep divisions in thinking between the adherents of these various theories, it seems necessary to provide at least a basic understanding, if not acceptance, of these concepts as they underlie our techniques.

HUMAN BEHAVIOR IS PURPOSIVE

Some may find it difficult to accept our theory that "all behavior is purposive" until they test the hypothesis. The teacher who sees Jimmy daydreaming in the classroom when he is supposed to be doing his lesson might well think that his behavior lacks purpose. If she did, however, she would be wrong. Jimmy's daydreaming fulfills a definite logical and coherent purpose for him, even though he may not be

[1] Rudolf Dreikurs, *Fundamentals of Adlerian Psychology*, Chicago, Alfred Adler Institute of Chicago, 1960.

aware of it, and possibly the teacher even less so. Each individual act has a goal or indicates a direction of movement. It is the goal of self-determined direction which motivates the child's behavior. He does not simply react to forces which impinge on him at any given moment, either from the outside world or within him. We see the individual actively interacting with his environment rather than passively responding to a given stimulus determining or causing his reactions.

BEHAVIOR IS THE RESULT OF OUR BIASED INTERPRETATION OF LIFE SITUATIONS

Whenever we act in a certain way, we act not in accordance with the reality of the situation as it confronts us, but according to our subjective appraisal of it. Our appraisal of any situation is subjective or biased and not necessarily in accord with reality—at least as others may perceive it—because we attach certain meanings to our experiences. We then make a preference and a decision based on these meanings. Because we can draw only on past knowledge from which to formulate present judgments, many of our interpretations are based on generalizations derived from experiences which occurred in our early childhood when we were unable to understand their meaning properly.

For example, a child may interpret his father's going on an extended business trip as a rejection of him, particularly if that has been a repeated occurrence and the child feels a lack of sufficient contact with the father. As most children are taught that withholding of affection is the consequence of misbehavior, a child may develop the erroneous assumption that father's reason for leaving is something that the child did that was wrong; consequently, the child may come to the generalization: "I must never risk attaching myself to anyone because they will leave me the first time I do something wrong," or "I must never do anything wrong or people will leave me and reject me." Repetition of such early experiences and consequent misinterpretation may lead to erroneous evaluations of similar situations even when the child reaches adulthood.

At the same time, it must be recognized that the subjectivity which leads to unavoidable mistakes in perception is also a necessity of our human functioning. Life is a continuous process of decision-making. Unfortunately, when confronted with the need to decide, we are almost never in possession of *all* the facts needed to aid us in making a truly objective choice. To complicate the matter further, we must also realize that even possession of all these facts does not guarantee an objective interpretation of them. Consequently, when it is necessary to act in order to meet the demands of our environment, we must make the best decision possible to us at the time. We must reduce that which is unintelligible to us to some sort of manageable order by a process which Adler called "the assumption of fictions." [2] To cite an example, he utilized our practice of drawing imaginary parallels and meridians on the globe to determine where we are at any given time. Though the lines do not really exist, by acting *as if* they do, we are able to determine quite precisely where we are, and in what direction may be our nearest geographical objective. If these assumptions are correct or nearly so, our ability to act is usually enhanced; however, if they are not in accord with reality (or with what may be considered reality by what is

[2] H. L. Ansbacher and R. R. Ansbacher, *The Individual Psychology of Alfred Adler,* New York, Basic Books, Inc., 1956.

called the "consensual validation" of a great majority of people), our acts may become confused, and we may do ourselves great harm.

Also, in making most of our decisions, we are not able to investigate the underlying conditions which are present. Accordingly, we act on assumptions and treat these assumptions *as if* they were real. As we become mature adults, we gradually develop the ability to evaluate *in advance* the possible consequences and to weigh the underlying facts which form the basis for our more crucial judgments. However, as Piaget [8] has pointed out so clearly, small children, because of their inability to interpret even empirical evidence objectively, must act constantly on many more mistaken judgments. The average 6-year-old child when confronted with a pound of chocolate in a single piece and the same weight in broken-up chunks, believes the latter to weigh more than the former. Most children at that age also "see" a quart of water in a tall jar as being more than the same amount in a flat container.

Thus, it is not the necessary *subjectivity* alone which hinders our development, but the inevitable *mistakes in perception* we make. If we had to stop and carefully weigh the evidence before taking a step, we would never learn to walk. We need assumed guiding lines to lead us through the complexity of social living. They are developed in early childhood on the strength of trial-and-error steps and often mistaken judgments.

One would assume that our perceptions are more likely to be in agreement with those of others when viewing inanimate objects. General semantics has demonstrated that this is not the case. Even when people talk about a table,

[8] Jean Piaget, *The Language and Thought of the Child*, London, Routledge and Kegan Paul, 1932.

their concept of what a table is may be quite different. These differences of perceptions are enhanced by our normal human biases. Ansbacher [4] observed that a group of poor children, when presented with colored chips simulating coins, considered the chips larger in size than did rich children, whose perceptions of them were more accurate. In our relationships with others, however, all of us tend to view interactions much more in accord with our biases than with reality. Each of us has a "private logic" which tells us to react to a given situation in the way we believe is best for us. Essentially, the process by which this private logic functions is rational and orderly even though the resulting behavior may not seem so to others. Our behavior may appear as irrational to those who do not know our biased apperception of the situation, which may be distorted. For example, the paranoid individual may erroneously believe that someone is out to kill or injure him. Though to most of us this premise is obviously in grave error, his attempts to meet this crisis are essentially quite logical and rational and follow a clearly defined pattern. Thus, in a similar fashion, if we are able to comprehend the steps by which a child develops his particular set of biased perceptions or apperceptions, whatever they may be, we may then better understand the immediate purposes of his behavior.

THE FUNDAMENTAL HUMAN MOTIVATION— THE NEED TO BELONG

It was Adler's postulation that man is primarily a social being. The need to belong or to be accepted is the basic human motivation. The child experiences this need through

[4] H. L. Ansbacher, "Adler's Place in the Psychology of Memory," *Journal of Personality,* Vol. 15, 1947, p. 200.

his helplessness and his awareness of dependence on others for the basic needs of life. This is first manifested in his connection with his mother and his perception of the relationship between her actions and the satisfactions of his physiological and emotional needs. However, he relates immediately to all other people in his environment, being influenced by them and influencing them in turn. Ultimately, this develops into a striving to function in and with a group in order to feel worthwhile or have significance.

Ideally, the child should discover that contributing to the welfare of the group is the best way to gain and maintain acceptance by others. However, only too frequently, through his biased apperceptions, the child fails to see that he can feel as a part of any group only if he contributes to the welfare of others—a contribution which ensures not only the survival of other members, but of himself as well.

DEVELOPMENT OF THE LIFE STYLE

Adler emphasized the holistic, unitary nature of personality. By this he meant that all the resources of the individual, his past experiences, present attitudes, and ideas of the future are utilized toward moving in a direction which gives him status and significances. Security means the feeling that one is worthwhile and has a place in the group.

The inevitable question arises, of course: "What about those who do not feel worthwhile or do not feel that they have a secure place in the group?" Their striving takes on a different form; yet it is still in the direction of attempting to find a place in the group and in society. The question can be categorized, in part, by placing Adler's concept of social interest at one extreme of a proposed continuum of belonging and placing exaggerated inferiority feelings at the other extreme. Thus, the fullest development of social interest might characterize the self-actualizing person as described by Maslow.[5] Such a person nearly always feels loved and wanted and accepted as a fully participating member of the group. In the cases which Maslow studied, the majority of individuals who represented this capacity devoted a substantial portion of their time contributing to the welfare of others. The opposite extreme might properly be represented by the psychotic who is so consumed by his feelings of inadequacy and inferiority as he compares himself to others that he withdraws almost completely from communication with the group. He still maintains his position in society, however, by forcing others to do things for him— sometimes even the most elementary functions, such as feeding him, clothing him, and providing him a place to live.

In one sense these two extreme individuals are alike: Both of them have developed a concept of what it is like to have a place in the group, and all their resources are devoted to maintaining and enhancing their position. The process by which both attempt to achieve the goals they have set for themselves is essentially consistent and quite logical, though their perceptions of the relationship between themselves and others are obviously quite different.

THE FICTIVE GOAL

At this point the next question might be: "How can two individuals utilizing a similar process arrive at such different conclusions about themselves and the world?" Adler's con-

[5] A. H. Maslow, *Motivation and Personality*, New York, Harper & Brothers, 1954.

cept regarding the development of the style of life furnishes us with some basic clues.

In his earliest formative months the child operates predominately by the process of trial and error. He makes random choices and watches their results. In the beginning he has little control over his responses; when he is happy he is happy all over, and when he is sad or angry all of his functions appear to operate accordingly. However, before long he learns to discriminate between one set of responses and another. He also learns that certain behavior brings certain actions from those around him—expressions of affection are generally met with a like behavior. Negative actions also have their counterpart. As a result, he gradually develops a repertoire of responses which are calculated to ensure physical and emotional satisfaction and avoid pain and punishment.

A behavioristic connotation of mere responses to stimulation and the child's development through a process of conditioning fails to recognize the active role which the child plays in his development. He always sizes up the situation and makes decisions, then anticipates the possible consequences and tries to prepare for them. This is not done on the conscious level of awareness; normal infants of deaf parents have been seen to cry without making any noise—realizing early the futility of such efforts.

This ability to anticipate may be perhaps the most important capacity which differentiates man from lower animals. Though animals do prepare for the future in certain ways, the evidence suggests that this is largely a matter of instinctual response to certain changes in climate and the chemical changes of their own bodies. However, as the child develops, he also gains an increasing awareness that these large beings around him who satisfy his wants also are in‹ terested in satisfying their own wishes. Accordingly, he begins to develop an idea of how to use their interests for his own benefit. Very early the child develops the capacity to manipulate the adults.

By the time he has reached four to six years of age he has a positive and detailed concept as to how he may reach a status of belonging and what role to play in the family. From then on this concept forms a mediating screen between himself and all the stimuli he subsequently receives. Each experience is evaluated in terms of the concept; accordingly, it is the *concept* rather than trial-and-error behavior which determines the ultimate direction of the child's response.

For example, let us consider the child who might have developed the idea that he can achieve a place in the group only by being special or the center of attention. He sees simple cooperation and sharing as distasteful because they do not emphasize his specialness. At this point all efforts of parents or teachers to stress the value of cooperation will fall on deaf ears.

If, on the other hand, the child feels relatively secure in his status with the group, he will be more concerned with enhancing the welfare of the group than his own. Accordingly, cooperation will seem to him a pleasant advantageous means of enhancing his status in the group.

THE LIFE STYLE

The life style has been postulated by Adler as being the sum total of the attitudes, goals, and beliefs the child developed in his attempt to find a place for himself. As they become established at a level of biased and inadequate awareness of reality, mistakes and faulty interpretations are unavoidable.

For example, the child who has always induced his parents to cater to his demands by crying or displays of temper, will likely develop the mistaken assumption that his place in the group will be assured as long as people serve him. As long as he succeeds in eliciting these responses he feels secure. When he does not get service and fulfillment of his wishes, he stops cooperating and feels inadequate and worthless. Moreover, as he has learned to interpret all actions of others in the light of whether they serve his demands or not, he sees demands for cooperation and sharing only as interfering with his needs. Then he stops his participation and switches to the "useless side." His convictions prevent him from recognizing his mistaken style of life, rather than seeing the error of his ways.

INFLUENCES THAT SHAPE THE DEVELOPMENT OF THESE CONCEPTS

The Inner Environment

The two influences which are most important in helping the child to shape his concept of himself in the world are his inner and outer environment. However, the objective dimensions of these environments are less important than how the child perceives them in his efforts to relate to the world.

The inner environment is primarily what the child experiences in his own body and the physical capacities with which he was born. They reflect his hereditary endowment and prenatal conditions and developments. A child born with a defect such as a deformed foot, for example, might view the world differently than if he had been born without such a defect. In his study of the effects of organ inferiorities, Adler [6] observed that what a child is born with is less important than what he does with it afterward. A study of three youngsters in an institution born with severe physical disability (*spina bifida,* an almost complete atrophy of the lower extremities) responded to their handicap in completely different ways.[7] One was bitter, revengeful, expressing his hatred and unhappiness very openly. The second was pleasant, well adjusted, neither striving too hard nor avoiding relationships and responsibilities. The third was a go-getter, highly ambitious, determined to go through college despite her handicap, lack of funds, and immobility. In each case, the handicap played an important role in motivation; but its significance depended on the decision of each youngster in which way he wanted to respond to it. Thus the age-old question of what is more important, heredity or environment, found a new answer. Their significance depends entirely on the child's interpretation and response to them. He is not, as one usually assumes, the victim of forces within and around him. It is he who determines their significance for *him and his* life.

The Outer Environment

In the outer environment, which consists of all the impressions the child receives from the outside world, his immediate family is the most important of the early influences.

6 Alfred Adler, *Study of Organ Inferiority and Its Psychical Compensation,* New York, The Nervous and Mental Disease Publishing Co., 1917.

7 Rudolf Dreikurs, "The Socio-Psychological Dynamics of Physical Disability," *Journal of Social Issues,* Vol. 4, 1948, pp. 39–54.

The family provides two kinds of experience about human relationships. *The family atmosphere* includes the ways and means by which the father and mother through their attitudes toward each other and their children pass on family and community standards and patterns to the children. If the parents are competitive and antagonistic toward one another, the children may grow up to believe this is to be expected of the world in general. If, however, the relationship between the parents is one of mutual love and respect, it will affect the relationships of all members of the family, and increase the children's opportunity to achieve a feeling of belonging.

We find that whatever is alike in all children of a given family generally reflects the family atmosphere. However, children may develop different traits and attitudes opposite to those set by the family atmosphere. These individual differences reflect competitive strife within the family constellation.[8]

The Family Constellation

Though the importance of parental attitudes in influencing the development of the child should not be minimized, the sibling relationships in the family often influence personality development of children more than their relationship to the parents. As early as 1929, Adler pointed to what was at that time a unique finding, the important effect which birth order had on the development of the child's concepts and personality.[9] Despite some similarities in the ways in which parents may treat their children, each child's position

[8] Rudolf Dreikurs, *The Challenge of Parenthood,* New York, Duell, Sloan & Pearce, 1948.

[9] Alfred Adler, *Problems of Neurosis,* New York, Cosmopolitan Book Corporation, 1930.

is different from that of any other sibling; therefore, his psychological field, his perception of himself and of the world around him is also different from that of his siblings. This sheds a good deal of light on the ways in which children develop.

The Oldest Child

The oldest child is for a time the sole object of parental attention. The arrival of another sibling constitutes a rude displacement or "dethronement," as Adler has termed it. Most of the child's subsequent efforts are devoted toward attempts to regain the position of being something special or seeking status through superiority. Corrective actions by the parents can help him to realize that he has a place in the family, regardless of the attention which his rival may receive. However, if he is unwilling to share, he may resort to seeking attention through misbehaviors and failure. There has been recent confirmation of Adler's views that the oldest child seems more prone to maladjustment and also tends to be more conservative, desiring to seek and keep power.[10]

The Second Child

The second child, on the other hand, has always had an older, often stronger and more capable pacemaker before him, whom he tries to overtake. If he succeeds in this—or if he finds a place for himself in a different and constructive direction—his development may be satisfactory. If, however, he feels that the older child has taken over the "good" role in the family, he may decide that destructiveness is his best way to gain the recognition he wants. Generally, how-

[10] Loren Grey, "An Analysis of the Eight Basic Theories of Alfred Adler Concerning the Development of the Child," unpublished Master's Thesis, University of Southern California, Los Angeles, 1954, p. 222.

ever, he is more daring and flexible than the first child and welcomes change, particularly if it might give him an advantage over his older rival.

In general, extreme differences in personality development are almost always present between the first two children. In most families each of them manages to find a different area of operation. Where one succeeds, the other gives up, and vice versa.[11] If the oldest child is a good student, the second child may shine socially or become an athlete or mechanic. If the older child is somewhat quiet and reserved, the second child may become an extrovert, and so on. Problems arise only if one or the other child despairs of ever competing successfully through constructive means, and therefore switches to the "useless side of life" (Adler) to take a destructive path.

The Middle Child

The second child becomes a middle child upon the birth of a third sibling; he often finds that the older child assumes the position of responsibility, and the youngest child that of the baby. Consequently, he often feels squeezed out. He does not have the rights of the older child nor the privileges of the younger. As a result of this interpretation, he may think that life is unfair and that there is no place for him, first in his family and then often in life.

The Youngest Child

The youngest child, though often babied and spoiled, appears to have a somewhat easier time of it than the others. He is never displaced. He either remains the baby for the rest of his life, or outdoes all the others. He usually gets the

[11] Rudolf Dreikurs and Vicki Soltz, *Children: The Challenge,* New York, Duell, Sloan & Pearce, 1964.

most attention and service, particularly if the older children become "substitute parents." Then he remains a "super-duper baby."

Large Families

In large families clear-cut differences in position can be seen not only in the oldest, the second, and the youngest child but in the group of the oldest, the babies, and so forth. The grouping is usually established on the basis of age. Of course other factors may enter. In large families one may see the first-second pattern repeated several times. Within each age group are the characteristic positions of an oldest, second, middle, or youngest child. These facts are important for teachers and parents as clues about the direction in which each child develops. With this knowledge they may help the child to move in a more constructive manner. The basic assumptions that each child develops in his family constellation are the basis for his personal "life style."

The Goals of Misbehavior

Unfortunately, our culture does not furnish sufficient means by which children can attain recognition through constructive activities. The methods used in raising children usually present them with a series of discouraging experiences. Consequently, all children try from time to time to solicit recognition by other means. We can find immediate goals behind every misbehavior or deficiency. All misbehavior is the result of a child's mistaken assumption about the way he can find a place and gain status. In order to deal with the misbehavior more effectively, the adult must be cognizant of its purpose and how the child uses it for his own benefit. When the adult is not aware of the meaning of the child's misbehavior, he responds by falling for the child's nonconscious scheme and thereby reinforces the child's mistaken goal. In order to deal more effectively with the child in the situation, the adult must vary his response.

We have identified four such goals underlying misbehaviors as: 1. Attention-getting; 2. struggle for power; 3. revenge; and 4. using disability as an excuse.

1. *Attention-getting*

This is by far the most common goal for most young children. It can be observed from time to time in the behavior of all children, and for that matter, in that of many adults. Getting attention is more often identified with disturbing behavior; but behind the cooperative behavior of very young children may often also be the desire for special attention. In fact, it is often extremely difficult to distinguish between behavior for the sake of attention-getting and cooperative behavior which stems from a genuine feeling of belonging and willingness to contribute. Generally speaking however, the "successful" child whose goal is attention-getting is trying to be the best, or better than the others. He is often a perfectionist, very sensitive to criticism, and fearful of failure. Like many other misguided children, he needs to realize that he does not require constant testimonials to prove his value and that satisfaction is inherent in the cooperative activity itself rather than in the favorable response it provokes.

However, at this point we are concerned primarily with the negative aspects of attention-getting behavior. There are innumerable ways by which this goal can be achieved. In classrooms it is the excessive talker, the squirmer, the child who refuses to stay in his seat, and the one who quarrels with his neighbors; it may also be the daydreamer and the procrastinator. At home such a child is "constantly getting into things," failing to do his chores, fighting with his siblings. He may be the dawdler, unable to dress or occupy himself. All of these disturbances and more are symptoms of the child's desire to get adults to pay attention to him, to serve him.

2. *Struggle for Power*

Often when a parent or teacher attempts to stop a misbehavior, which originally was for attention only, a power struggle ensues. In this situation the child tries to control the situation or the adult, rather than to solicit attention. While the child often does not ultimately win in such a struggle, he scores a "victory" each time he can defeat an order or command. Thus, the parent or teacher who allows himself to get into an argument with the child, trying to force compliance of his demands, experiences endless "defeats." In fact, he is actually playing into the child's hands. *Once the battle has been joined, the child has already won it.*

3. *Revenge*

The child whose behavior is motivated by revenge manifests a level of disturbance which borders on the pathologic. Generally, this is reached only after a long series of discouragements where the child has decided that attention-getting and power will not serve to compensate him for his utter lack of a sense of belonging. The child bent on revenge has given up every hope of attaining any worthiness through constructive activities. Essentially, he has reached the stage where he thinks everyone is against him, and the only way to get recognition is to retaliate against adults for the way he feels he has been treated. Usually he is right in his interpretation; he *is* pushed around. (He just does not realize how his offensive behavior almost compels the kind of treatment he receives.)

As can readily be seen, the behavior of most delinquent children is an expression of this goal. Generally, they feel that the only way they can be recognized is by provoking hostility. This leads to punitive activities by society, which in turn provokes further hostility from the delinquent. The end result of this unhappy cycle is all too often the habitual criminal who feels only the urge to commit further crimes as soon as he is released from prison. He is fighting with society and is willing to accept the fortunes of war.

4. *Disability as an Excuse*

Perhaps the most extreme form of discouragement is manifested in the use of assumed disability or a display of inadequacy. The child has given up every effort in the given area; he wants little more than to be left alone so that his deficiency then may not be so painfully obvious. However, we often find relatively well-functioning individuals who assume disabilities in specific areas, though not as total failures. An assumed inadequacy in mathematics is one of the common forms of this phenomenon. However, we are more concerned with the child who has assumed disability or inadequacy as a *total behavior pattern*. We have stated previously:

> No defeat will stop the child's efforts as long as he considers it only as temporary and sees hope for eventual success. In this sense failure and defeat may sometimes stimulate special effort and actually cause spectacular successes. When hope of success is given up, the full force of discouragement comes into play. When a child will reach the conclusion that it is hopeless to try cannot be predicted; but the consequences become evident immediately; and it is often the

misguided corrective efforts of a parent or teacher which convinced the child of the hopelessness of his efforts. He may seek success in other areas, or more often strive for attention, power, status in new and unacceptable fields of endeavor. But the crucial factor is that he has abandoned efforts in certain areas, which may remain weak spots for the rest of his life. This is an important fact: most educators overlook the remaining areas of discouragement if a child succeeds in finding areas of special achievement. They usually assume that his talents are limited to these fields and do not realize that preference for certain activities is often the consequence of discouragement in others.[12]

THE IMPORTANCE OF EXPECTANCY

Underlying all the interactions previously described are the expectations of the child. Every child—or adult for that matter—acts according to the way he expects things will happen. Most adults respond to the child's expectations and thereby reinforce his behavior. Thus, if a child who repeatedly talks in a class is scolded and told to be quiet, this procedure, instead of teaching him to behave differently in the future, rather reinforces his approach. Similarly, the revengeful child who provokes hostility from others does so because he wants and expects them to abuse him so that he can feel justified in what he does.

In other words, in order to understand the child's actions, one has to see them in the total field, not as emanating from the child, but being part of the total situation in which the child, his peers, his parents, and his teachers all cooperate to give meaning to what he does, whether it is right or wrong.

[12] Don Dinkmeyer and Rudolf Dreikurs, *Encouraging Children to Learn: The Encouragement Process*, Englewood Cliffs, N.J., Prentice-Hall, 1963, p. 42.

CHAPTER 3

Principles Involved in the New Tradition

Raising children has always been based on tradition. Few people realize the cultural abnormality of our times. Unlike other species on this earth, our generation of adults needs lectures, books, and instruction about what to do with their young. Usually each generation learns this from the preceding one. Margaret Mead [1] has described a number of primitive societies, each of which raised children in different ways and brought about the development of specific personality types; but in each tribe children were probably raised in the same way for thousands of generations, and each adult and each child knew what to do in certain complex situations. It is the advent of democracy which caused the present dilemma. It happened before in ancient Rome and Greece when Cicero and Plato complained about the children's lack of respect for their elders. A similar democratic period, with its change in human relationships, caused the educational difficulties during the last few centuries. In the democratic evolution with its increased degree of equality, each new generation of children gained more freedom and successfully challenged to an increasing degree the au-

[1] Margaret Mead, *From the South Seas,* New York, William Morrow & Company, 1939.

thority of its elders. Today we can no longer "make" a child behave, study, or apply himself.

The most outstanding feature of the new ways needed in dealing with children is the realization that pressure from without has lost its effectiveness. One can no longer subdue children with bribe and threat. Reward and punishment were effective in an autocratic setting. Today if we give a reward, the child no longer accepts that gratefully as a favor of a benevolent authority. No, he regards it as his right, and he will not do anything unless another reward is forthcoming. The situation is even worse in regard to punishment. The only children who respond well to it are those who would not need it, with whom one could reason. Those whom we try to impress with punitive consequences may respond for a short moment, and then resume their defiance. They feel that if the adult has the right to punish them, they have the same right too. And mutual retaliations fill our homes and schools. The first step toward a new educational policy must be the realization that one cannot hope for good results through punishment. It has to be replaced by the application of logical or natural consequences where the child is impressed with the needs of reality and not with the power of an adult.

STIMULATION INSTEAD OF PRESSURE

The traditional autocratic approach of motivating children through pressure from without must be replaced with stimulation from within. Parents and teachers alike must become familiar with new devices. They are new only in the sense that they are usually unknown, although educators for the last few centuries, as was pointed out in a previous chapter, were promoting similar approaches. The basic principle in dealing with each other as equals is a relationship based on mutual respect. Our children have become our equals, not in size, skills, or experience, but in their right and ability to decide for themselves instead of yielding to a superior power. Most mistakes in dealing with children are due to the lack of mutual respect, needed in dealing with equals. Conflicts of interest and desire will always exist as long as people live together. In the past such conflicts were resolved by the one who was strongest; the weaker merely had to submit. Today such simple solutions of conflicts are no longer effective. The loser immediately challenges—and often successfully—the decision imposed upon him. When parents and teachers experience a conflict with the child, they usually proceed by either fighting or giving in. If they fight, they violate respect for the child, and if they give in, they neglect respect for themselves. But most educators do not know what else to do. This is the main problem of the emerging new tradition in dealing with children: how not to fight without giving in. It is possible to do so if one becomes familiar with the many ways by which children can be stimulated to meet the needs of the situation and to resolve conflicts through agreement. The best formula for the proper attitude toward children is to treat them with kindness and with firmness. Kindness expresses respect for the child and firmness evokes respect from the child. There are people who are kind but not firm, and others who are firm but not kind. Many are kind and firm, but seldom at the same time.

TECHNIQUES VERSUS ATTITUDES

Parents and teachers ask for help in their task of influencing children. They want to know what they should do. They are sincere in this inquiry, but they are seldom given an answer. We find a tendency not to take the question seriously. Because many of those who are consulted really do not know what to advise, they consider giving advice as improper. They maintain that any parent or teacher who is mature, emotionally stable, who has the correct attitude toward children does not need any advice, and the rest would not be able to benefit from it. Consequently, we find the literature filled with generalities, which often are erroneous or have little practical value. Telling a mother that her difficulties with her child is the consequence of her lack of love is, in most cases, an unwarranted insult, and not even correct. The mother may have a deep love for her child; but if she does not know what to do with him and feels constantly defeated, she may be so upset that she may not be able to show her love. What is worse, the desire to give love induces many mothers to spoil the child. All generalities like the advice to have more patience, to give more love and security, are usually meaningless because the parents don't know how to be more patient and have more love.

The proper attitude of a parent and teacher is not a *premise* for being effective, but rather its *consequence*. When the mother discovers how she can influence the child and win his cooperation, her attitude begins to change. It is not infrequent that the mother then for the first time really can enjoy the child of whom she has been afraid. The same holds true for the teacher. The good teacher knows what to do with the child. But she is good because she knows, although she usually has not learned in college what to do. She merely is one of those "naturals" who senses what the child needs, through her empathy and not through her training. At the present time teachers do not learn what to do with a child who misbehaves or refuses to study. They do not want, in most cases, to be autocratic, but they do not know how to be democratic. Neither parents nor teachers are prepared to deal with the child as an equal. They need information about the methods which are effective in a democratic setting. Every mother and every teacher can learn what to do if they want to, regardless of how disturbed they may be. Helping them requires such specific recommendations that anyone who has the desire to test them can acquire the skill and can learn to apply the technique. In this regard our approach is often in contrast to prevalent forms of advice and counseling.

The principles for exerting beneficial and corrective influences on the child are the same for parents and for teachers. And yet each has different opportunities. We constantly encounter the question as to whose obligation it is to improve a child's deficiencies and maladjustment. It is characteristic of our time, with its cultural ignorance about educational effectiveness, that each blames the other for the shortcomings of the child and requests the other to correct him. We find this typical situation between father and mother. The less the mother knows what to do with the child, the better she knows what father should do, and vice versa. Passing the buck is the tacit admission of one's inability to find answers to the child's problems. Actually, anyone who understands the child and can win his cooperation can help him in his improvement and adjustment, whether a parent, a teacher, a relative, a friend of the family, a minister, or a youth leader. The parents certainly have it in their reach to change a child's behavior, particularly if he is young. They can use many approaches which the classroom situation does not permit. On the other hand, the teacher has the great advantage of working with the group. And the group can exert stronger influences on children than any adult. As the authority of the adults diminishes, the influence of the peer group increases, particularly when the child reaches adolescence. Because of the inadequate training of our present generation of teachers, few realize that a teacher can correct all the wrong influences of the home and of the community because she can use the group to exert its influence on each individual child.

It is not within the premise of this book to present in detail the many approaches and techniques by which adults can change the motivation of the child, or even—what is more important—help him to grow up without encountering unnecessary deficiencies and failures. We will present in this book one of the most effective and, yet at the same time, most complex approaches: the application of logical and natural consequences. However, in order to understand the significance of this corrective measure, it is necessary to see its relationship to the many other influences which adults can exert in a democratic setting and which they need to know.

PARENT EDUCATION

The need for parent education is widely recognized; the methods of obtaining it vary a great deal. Alfred Adler and his associates have made considerable contributions to provide the necessary information to parents. Besides giving classes and organizing parent-counseling centers for the demonstration of effective ways of raising children, they have published many books on this subject.[2] Most recently we published thirty-four principles which parents need to know to become effective in dealing with their children.[3] A review of some may indicate the great variety of means by which children can be redirected. Some of the principles can be applied by the teacher as well; others lend themselves only to an application within the home.

One of the most important corrective influences is *encouragement*. Every misbehaving child is discouraged and needs continuous encouragement, just as a plant needs water and sunshine. The art of encouragement is not easy to acquire, because we are all prone to discourage others and ourselves. As has been stated before, reward and punishment are outdated. Natural and logical *consequences* replace the punitive retaliation; their application requires considerable skill and sensitivity. The child requires firmness. But firmness must avoid domination, otherwise it does not evoke respect, but rebellion. One cannot be firm if one talks. In the moment of conflict, talking is increased warfare and can have no beneficial effect. In a conflict situation, one must withdraw from the conflict, since one only increases counteraction through the efforts to fight it out. One must withdraw from the child's provocation but not from

2 Alfred Adler, *The Problem Child,* New York, G. P. Putnam's Sons, 1963; Marguerite Beecher and Willard Beecher, *Parents on the Run,* New York, Julian Press, 1955; Rudolf Dreikurs, *The Challenge of Parenthood,* New York, Duell, Sloan & Pearce, 1948; Erwin Wexberg, *Our Children in a Changing World,* New York, The Macmillan Company, 1938.

3 Rudolf Dreikurs and Vicki Soltz, *Children: The Challenge,* New York, Duell, Sloan & Pearce, 1964.

the child. The child needs much attention and recognition but not when he tries to gain it through misbehavior and deficiency. Preaching, explaining, and advising are usually useless since the child knows that he is doing wrong. Through disinvolvement one can impress the child with the futility of his disturbing behavior, but in order to be able to use the extremely powerful method of withdrawal, one must first realize the goal of the child, the purpose of his transgression, whether a desire to attract attention, to show his power, to hurt and get even, or to display his deficiency in order to be left alone. A temper tantrum becomes meaningless if there is no audience. Few parents realize that most fights between the children are for the parents' benefit. The children learn fast to settle their squabbles if left to their own devices.

Unless parents take time out for training the child, they will spend much more time with the disturbances created by an untrained child. Criticism and emphasis of mistakes does not evoke growth. It is necessary to win the child's cooperation; one cannot demand it, one must earn it, like confidence and trust. One of the most important first steps for a mother is to learn to be quiet, not to talk. Talking is extremely ineffective and usually makes the child "mother-deaf." One cannot train the child to take on responsibility— one must *give* it to him. Overprotection has the same discouraging effect as humiliation; it deprives the child of the experience of his own strength. Adults must watch for their first impulse when the child misbehaves. It usually is exactly what the child wants to get, and it thereby reinforces only his mistaken goal.

Many new methods seem to contradict accepted standards. Increasing the competition between siblings by treating each one as he deserves, the good and the bad, only intensifies their intentions. The good will be good only because he wants to be better and the bad one finds his approach gratifying in gaining status and power. Only if one treats the children as a group and lets all take the responsibility for whatever any one of them is doing wrong, can we make the children realize that each one *is* his brother's keeper.

Another difficult principle is the realization of the harm done when one feels sorry for a child. It is only a natural reaction if a child has been exposed to unfortunate experiences. However, observation shows that the pity and sympathy of well-meaning friends and relatives often does much more harm than the predicament which had evoked this reaction. If one feels sorry for the child, regardless of how justifiable such emotional reaction may be, one teaches the child that he has the right to feel sorry for himself; and nobody is as miserable as one who feels sorry for himself. Besides that, it gives the child the impression that life owes him something and that he has the right to demand more and more, an attitude which undermines greatly the child's ability to participate and to contribute.

Many parents find it difficult to believe that a child's fears are a means of getting special consideration and service. They do not express a child's insecurity, as is usually assumed. The child's fear will vanish when the parents, in a quiet way, show understanding but no special concern. The same holds true for a so-called dependent child. He has no "dependency needs." A dependent child is always a tyrant who uses real or assumed weaknesses to put others in his service. He can become independent and self-reliant in the shortest period of time when the parents, mostly the mother, stop giving service and assistance.

One of the most important institutions in a democratic family is the family council. At present the children feel free to do as they please, and the adults have to take on the consequences. It is difficult for most parents to sit down with their children as equal partners to discuss the problems of the family together and to find means by which they all can solve them. But unless the technique of conducting regular family council sessions has been acquired, smooth functioning of the family is almost impossible, since everyone is inclined to think only of himself, his wishes, his needs, his intentions. It is particularly difficult for the mother to share the responsibility for what goes on in the family. The concept of a "good" mother is that she alone has the duty to see that everything goes well. Giving up this manipulating position only too frequently appears to a mother as failing on her job. This picture of a loving, giving, responsible mother is fortified by professional and lay people alike. Without this overwhelming feeling of responsibility and the inevitable fear of neglecting her duty, motherhood could become so much more enjoyable and children so much more independent and responsible.

THE CHANGING ROLE OF THE TEACHER

The controversy still rages whether it is the teacher's task mainly to instruct; any assumption that she should be burdened with the task of helping the child in his adjustment is rejected with vehemence. The teacher is often hardly capable of imparting knowledge because of large classes and an increasing number of reluctant learners. It seems unreasonable to give her a further assignment. As a matter of fact, if the teacher is not able to change the motivation of children, overcoming their individual academic and social deficiences, then she is hardly in a position to "teach" effectively. If she cannot take the time needed to influence the behavior and attitude of a disturbing child, then she has to spend a great deal more time with the maladjusted and defiant student. It is not sufficient that the teacher knows her subject and the principles of education. This was sufficient in an autocratic society where the children had to conform, whether they liked it or not, or face dire consequences. Today, if the child does not want to study, trying to force him only increases his reluctance. Unfortunately, the less the child is interested in studying, the more unpleasant we make it for him, through imposed homework, punishment, poor grades, and similar weapons. To overcome the present educational impasse, we need not only drastic revisions of the curriculum, but training for teachers in psychodynamics and group dynamics. Such training does not imply a greater burden on the teacher, but, on the contrary, can make her teaching assignment not only more effective but also more enjoyable. Presently, she learns little about what to do with a child who does not want to study or to behave well. The time required for such training is minimal in contrast to the benefits it provides.

UNDERSTANDING THE CHILD

We do not need to leave understanding to the degree of sensitivity which a teacher incidentally acquired in her own personal development. The teleoanalytic approach, which considers behavior as purposive, can enable any teacher who becomes acquainted with it to understand the child and his actions. This does not make her a psychologist or psychotherapist; but it permits her to apply effective psychological approaches in her classroom.[4]

There are three approaches which permit the teacher to acquire the necessary sensitivity to diagnose the child's goals and motivation. The first is mere observation. By observing the reactions which the child evokes, it is often obvious whether he disturbed to get attention (goal 1), to demonstrate his power (goal 2), to hurt (goal 3), or to be left alone (goal 4). If the teacher is uncertain about her diagnosis, she can verify it by what is called the "corrective feedback." If a child talks out of turn, gets out of his seat, is noisy or disturbs in any other way, he can do that either to keep the teacher busy or to defy and defeat her. By trying to stop him, the difference of motivation usually becomes manifest. If the child merely was bidding for teacher's attention, he will stop his disturbance when she reprimands him—although not for long, since he constantly wants to keep her busy. However, his reaction will be quite different if his disturbance is part of his plan to defeat her, to show that he can do as he pleases. If she tells him to stop, he will not only not stop, but increase his disturbance. Then the teacher can see with what she is confronted.

The third, and most reliable, means to diagnose the child's goal is at the same time the most distressing aspect of the teacher-child relationship. Whenever a child creates a disturbance either actively or passively, the teacher can watch her own emotional reaction and her impulse. If she is annoyed by the child's actions or deficiencies, she can be

[4] Rudolf Dreikurs, *Psychology in the Classroom*, New York, Harper & Row, rev. ed., 1967.

pretty certain that he wanted to keep her busy with him. If she feels provoked and angry, trying to show him that he cannot do that to her, she is only falling into his bid for power and providing him with the opportunity to show her that he *can*. And if she feels deeply hurt by what the child does, the chances are that she is only doing what he wants, mainly feeling hurt. And if she feels like throwing up her arms in despair, because she does not know what to do with him, then she probably does exactly what he wants her to do, to give up and leave him alone.

The sad fact is that the teacher not only responds to the child's scheme, but reinforces it by following her first impulse. Until all teachers will be able to understand the child's motivation and goals, they are bound to succumb to the child's unconscious scheme, and then are surprised that their corrective efforts fail.[5]

PSYCHOLOGICAL APPROACHES

We have to distinguish the specific particularly from the nonspecific methods. Certain approaches are specifically designed for an individual child who disturbs or is deficient. More effective are nonspecific methods which can, and should, be applied to all problems which arise in the classroom. Nevertheless, we will try to outline briefly the first steps a teacher should take when she becomes aware of the child's goals.

In all cases a teacher needs to become disinvolved, which is just the opposite of what she usually does. If the child tries to keep her busy, then it is obvious that her scolding, nag-

[5] Rudolf Dreikurs, "Do Teachers Understand Children?" *School and Society,* February, 1959.

ging, and so forth will not stop him, but encourage him to continue his successful maneuver. The teacher does not have it as easy as the parent who can just leave the child alone. However, she can ignore his disturbance, at least on the verbal level. To wait until he is quiet, implies the use of the group as a pressure. There are many ways by which the teacher can demonstrate to the child that his annoyance does not pay off for him. Without going into more details, the teacher can confront the child with his goals in a private session, or in group discussions. She can make a pact with him and agree on the number of times he would want her special attention, and then merely call the number. Sometimes, to stop talking and look at him may be sufficient. Certain logical consequences may be applicable and will be discussed later. The main line of procedure should be minimizing the attention for disturbing forms of behavior and replacing them with special attention given to the child for constructive actions, until he no longer needs attention as a means of finding his place. This requires the application of encouragement.

In a power struggle the first requirement is disinvolvement. The teacher may feel obliged to impose her restraining will on the child. She is afraid of losing status and respect in the class if she does not do so. But she is in error in this assumption. Nothing is as pathetic as a defeated authority who does not want to admit defeat. An open admission that the child is stronger and that she cannot "make" him stop, actually enhances her influence in the class. There is not much fun in showing one's power if the power is not contested. Again, confrontation of the child with his goals, particularly in group discussion, is essential. The teacher can stop her work until the child complies with what he knows he should do and the class can exert the necessary influence much more effectively than can the teacher. No teacher is obliged to fight with a child unless she decides to do so. If she does, she will inevitably be the loser, regardless of any temporary victory she may score. At the present time the provocation by power-drunk children is one of the greatest and most frequent threats to our educational programs.

The child who wants to hurt can be vicious; he knows how to hit below the belt. To convince him that one does not fall for his scheme is extremely difficult since he is so clever in his devices that one usually cannot help but feel hurt. Here a long process is needed to convince such a child that he can be liked and accepted, that he has a chance to gain status through useful means. It requires great skill to convey to the child trust and understanding without antagonizing the rest of the class. The teacher will need the help of the class to overcome the hostility of such children and to draw them into a constructive partnership.

With the completely discouraged child who has given up hope and expectancy of success, encouragement is the specific need. Without it no improvement will be possible, regardless of how much effort may be expended, both on the part of the teacher and the child himself.

ENCOURAGEMENT

Skill in encouraging students is a prerequisite for any effective corrective effort. In many cases the consequences of the teacher's actions will depend largely on their inherent quality of encouragement or discouragement. If the teacher's actions contribute to further discouragement of the child, then she has done harm, regardless of how justified and understandable her actions may have been. One can safely say that most efforts of teachers in dealing with the reluctant learner or the defiant rebel are discouraging, despite the best intention of the teacher. It requires either an unusual kind of person who can exert an encouraging influence on anyone with whom she comes in contact, or to learn this intricate and complex procedure called encouragement. The art of encouragement should be a mandatory subject for the training of all teachers. This is the reason why we undertook to provide a text for such a class.[6]

Essentially, encouragement involves the ability to accept the child as worthwhile, regardless of any deficiency, and to assist him in developing his capacity and potentialities. Unfortunately, though the principle of providing encouragement is widely accepted, few understand thoroughly the nature of the process and often discourage without meaning to do so. Specifically, the person who encourages: (1) places value on the child as he is; (2) shows faith in the child and enables him to have faith in himself; (3) sincerely believes in the child's ability and wins his confidence while building his self-respect; (4) recognizes a job "well done," gives recognition for effort; (5) utilizes the group to facilitate and enhance the development of the child; (6) integrates the group so that each student can be sure of his place in it; (7) assists in the development of the skills sequentially and psychologically based to permit success; (8) recognizes and focuses on strength and assets; and (9) utilizes the interest of the child to energize instruction.[7]

---

[6] Don Dinkmeyer and Rudolf Dreikurs, *Encouraging Children to Learn: The Encouragement Process*, Englewood Cliffs, N.J., Prentice-Hall, 1963, p. 50.

[7] *Ibid.*, p. 50.

Encouragement, while not a specific approach but important in dealing with all children, is still a psychological procedure, an application of psychological principles in dealing with the child. The same holds true for the application of logical and natural consequences. They are equally complex and require considerable skill and training to be applied effectively. But they provide some of the strongest means of changing the child's motivation. The rest of this book will be devoted to the discussion of this approach. There is a peculiar link between encouragement and the use of logical consequences. There are many who are inclined to consider both as nothing but the old principle of reward and punishment. And truly, under the disguise of encouragement and application of consequences, the unskilled teacher can use them like reward and punishment; but then he will not gain the benefits of either. There is a fundamental difference between reward and encouragement. They have in common a friendly attitude, and therefore seem to be identical. However, they are different both in timing and in their effect. The reward is usually given to a child for something well done, for some achievement, regardless of how small it may be. Encouragement is needed when the child fails. Many assume that this can be achieved by providing the child with successes and then rewarding him for them. Few realize that success can be most discouraging. First, the child may come to the conclusion that he did succeed once, but could not do it again. His recent "success" may become a threat for his future ability to succeed. But what is worse, such a procedure conveys to the child the assumption, which actually is shared by most of his teachers and fellow students, that he is worthwhile only when he is successful. This attitude is so widely accepted that its fundamentally discouraging effect is hardly noticed.

Similarly, unskilled educators, parents, and teachers alike, are inclined to use "consequences" in form of a punitive retaliation. Under these circumstances, the best possible consequence is turned into an ineffective punishment. The tone of voice alone often distinguishes one from the other. There is often a fine line between both, perhaps not perceived by the adult with his diminished sensitivity, but well understood by the children who respond accordingly.

SOCIAL INTEGRATION

Even more important than an understanding of the individual child and of his motivation is the social setting in which he acts and behaves in his unique way. This explains the excellent results many teachers achieve with their students without any training and information about psychodynamics. They merely create the atmosphere in which each child can play a constructive role, and use their leadership qualities to integrate the class for a common purpose. The need for such integration has received far too little attention in the past. One of the principal reasons for this deficiency was the fallacious assumption that the teacher has single-handedly to teach, control, and correct each individual child in the class. Under this assumption, the size of the class became an important factor, usually in a negative sense. The teacher felt unable to give what she considered the necessary personal attention to each child.

In actuality, a teacher does not teach twenty, thirty, or forty students who happen to sit in one class. She teaches only *one* class, which may consist of twenty, thirty, or forty students. The difference between these two divergent perceptions of the teacher's role is immense and crucial. As long as the teacher is concerned with each child, she constantly neglects the others when she is occupied with one. As a consequence, the question is often raised to what extent a teacher can sacrifice the interest of the whole class for her preoccupation with one disturbing child. The teacher who is aware of the fact that she is always dealing with one group, and who is capable of exerting group leadership, will not encounter such a contingency. Each child is an integral part of the whole class, regardless of the role he may play in it. If the teacher can exert her leadership and thereby becomes capable of integrating the class, then the disturbing child can serve to activate the other students, thereby becoming an asset, while the other children can learn to help him.

It is the obligation of a leader to create the proper atmosphere in her group. Our teachers, by and large, are not trained in the various ways in which group leadership can be exerted. The example Kurt Lewin gave in his Iowa experiments [8] is almost completely forgotten. He demonstrated the different group climates created by leaders who are either autocratic, democratic, or laissez-faire anarchic. Our teachers want to be democratic, which may be the consequence of the strong influence of Dewey on American education. But they simply do not know how to be democratic, and often consider the democratic leadership as a form of anarchy, where everybody can do what he wants. Even when they try to correct the ensuing anarchy through dictatorial approaches, they do not even know how to be good autocrats. The differences between autocratic and

[8] Kurt Lewin, *Resolving Social Conflicts*, New York, Harper & Brothers, 1948.

democratic leadership are well known and described.[9] Without the teacher's ability to be a democratic leader, she cannot exert much influence: She is either overpermissive or dominating; neither way is effective in influencing the class.

It is not the place here to give the details of democratic leadership, of the various means by which teachers can integrate the whole class and lead it to a mutually accepted educational goal. The ability to create a cooperative and stimulating atmosphere cannot be left to the personal attributes and abilities of each teacher. All have to learn and can develop the skills needed for such purpose. At the present time most classes are divided in two or more camps. There is first the teacher versus the class, and then various subgroups opposing each other, some siding with the teacher, some working against her.

We witness a tendency to resolve this dilemma by creating homogeneous classes, mostly according to ability but also in regard to conformity or rebellion. All such attempts are bound to fail. The teacher who has learned how to be a good group leader can integrate even a highly heterogenous class, as many examples have shown. And if the teacher lacks such an ability, the most homogeneous class will still not function as a whole, but be divided by success, sex, attitudes, and values of the students. They need leadership to function as a group.

GROUP DISCUSSION

A democratic classroom permits the students to share the responsibility for functioning and progress with the teacher. In a democratic era we can no longer succeed in having schools run by adults *for* the students; we need to have the

---

[9] Dreikurs, *Psychology in the Classroom,* p. 74.

students as partners. In each class the cooperation of the students and the integration of all require regular group discussion in which the problems of the class and of each member are freely discussed. Such group discussions are needed from the early elementary grades up. However, few teachers are trained in conducting effective group discussions. They either use them to impose their ideas on the students, or they let the students talk without taking any leadership. Democracy requires leadership. The teacher as leader can use the group first to give everyone a chance to express himself and to be sure to be heard, second to understand each other better, and third to help each other in achieving the educational goal. An essential by-product of such regular and frank group discussions is the opportunity for the teacher to influence the thinking and the values of his students which may now differ greatly from those which are considered beneficial. Group discussions alone can bridge the gap between the various opposing forces within the class. A democratic classroom organization, recognizing the present status of equality and freedom for all, is impossible without regular discussions.

These various aspects of our present educational systems, the family and the school, should provide the background and the frame of reference in which one of the most potent correctional methods, the application of natural and logical consequences, can be applied. They are no cure-all. Some believe that natural consequences have to be applied every moment as a gimmick to induce conformity and compliance. While the "consequences" cannot serve as a tool to force children into submission, they can be of crucial value, but only in a truly democratic setting, replacing the authority of the adults with the reality of the situation.

CHAPTER 4

The Concept of Logical Consequences

WHAT IS A LOGICAL CONSEQUENCE?

The formulation of the term *logical consequence* arose out of the need to describe correctly activities which cannot strictly be categorized as natural consequences. However, in order to understand both concepts, it is first necessary to explain what is meant by a natural consequence.

To do this we must recognize the logic of behavior which seems to characterize the activities of all living organisms. In order to survive, all living beings must function in a way which is compatible in some degree to their environmental conditions. If they do not act in this way they die. Applying this to human behavior, we can assume that no one will willingly do what he believes is not good for himself: that is, nothing which does not, in his eyes, ensure status and survival. To give some examples: If a man is walking along the street and he trips on a raised edge in the sidewalk, the next time he passes that same spot he will usually be more cautious and step over. A child who puts his hand on a hot stove and burns it will avoid such unpleasantness in the future. It follows that every act has a consequence, and if we are to avoid unpleasant results of our acts we must then behave in a way which will help to guarantee more favorable results. The term *natural consequences* has been defined as denoting the natural results of ill-advised acts. If the results are unpleasant, they may lead to an avoidance of these acts in the future, unless there is some—often veiled—benefit in their continuation.

ORIGINS OF THE TERM
NATURAL CONSEQUENCES

More than a hundred years ago Herbert Spencer first clearly saw the implications of this method for child rearing. He was concerned with the arbitrary use of punishment of children by adults, though there was little evidence to indicate that he regarded such punishments as not being based on parental understanding of the moral issues of the day. Regarding punishment, he said:

> It is forgotten that in the carrying out of any such system presupposes on the part of adults the degree of intelligence or goodness or self-control possessed by no one. The error made by those who discuss questions of domestic discipline lies in describing all the faults and difficulties of the children and none of the parents. . . . The truth is that the difficulties in lower education are necessarily of dual origin and necessarily result from the combined faults of the parents and children.[1]

Spencer, in support of Rousseau's concepts of a hundred years earlier, also condemned the excessively harsh treatment accorded many children by parents and adults, which in his view tended to debase them rather than to prepare them for the demands of adult life:

[1] Herbert Spencer, *Education—Intellectual, Moral, Physical,* New York, P. D. Alden Publ., 1885, pp. 154–156.

Instead of being an aid to human progress, which all culture should be, the culture of our public schools by accustoming boys to the despotic form of government and an intercourse regulated by a brutal force tends to fit them for a lower state of society than that which exists; and chiefly recruited, as our legislature is, from among those brought up in such schools, a barbarizing influence becomes a hindrance to national progress.[2]

In his discussions regarding a more proper corrective for childhood misbehaviors, Spencer discusses first the concept of what we might consider a true natural consequence:

> When a child falls or runs his head against a table, it suffers a pain, the remembrance of which tends to make it more careful; and by repetition of such experiences, it is eventually disciplined into proper guidance of its movements. ... So deep an impression is produced by one or two events of this kind, that no persuasion will afterwards induce it thus to disregard the laws of its constitution. ...
>
> Note in the second place, the character of the punishments by which these physical transgressions are prevented. Punishments, we call them, in absence of a better word; for they are not punishments in the literal sense. They are not artificial and unnecessary inflictions of pain; but are simply the beneficient checks to actions which are at variance with bodily welfare—checks in the absence of which life would be quickly destroyed by bodily injuries. It is the peculiarity of these penalties, if we must so call them, that they are simply the *unavoidable consequences* of the deeds which they follow: are nothing more than the *inevitable reactions* entailed by the child's actions.[3]

In this we can see his exposition of what happens when the child violates a rule of what might be called the natural

[2] *Ibid.*, p. 158.
[3] *Ibid.*, pp. 161–163.

order. At the same time, Spencer also appeared to be clearly aware of the possible application of this process to situations involving disturbance of what we call the social order, as well.

NATURAL VERSUS LOGICAL CONSEQUENCES

In his discussions of the concept of natural consequences, however, Spencer did not particularly discriminate between those acts where the consequences were solely the result of the child's own action, and those where consequences were more or less arranged by parents or other adults. It was here that the need for a more definitive description of the process developed. We have suggested the term logical consequences to define situations where the consequence is, in effect, arranged by the parent or another adult rather than being solely the result of the child's own acts.[4] To give an example, the consequences of a child's putting his hand on the hot stove would be considered a natural consequence. However, Spencer's suggested corrective procedure to be followed by the parent might more properly be considered a logical rather than a natural consequence:

Having refused or neglected to pick up and put away the things that children scattered about and thereby having entailed the trouble of doing this on someone else, the child should, on subsequent occasions, be denied the means of giving this trouble. When it next petitions for the toybox, the reply of its mamma should be, "The last time you had your toys you left them lying on the floor and Jane had to pick them up. Jane is too busy to pick up every day the things you leave around and I cannot do it myself, so if

[4] Rudolf Dreikurs and Vicki Soltz, *Children: The Challenge,* New York, Duell, Sloan & Pearce, 1964, p. 84.

you will not put your toys away when you are done with them, I cannot let you have them." [5]

Though the consequence of the act is that the child who has neglected to put his toys away cannot use them, the result has been arranged by the mother. However, in order for it to be effective, it must be *experienced* by the child as logical in nature, or the corrective effect may be lost. That is, of course, where the crux of the matter lies and where a careful explanation of the psychological basis for logical consequences should be made.

DIFFERENCES BETWEEN LOGICAL OR NATURAL CONSEQUENCES AND PUNISHMENT

Punishment is as old as human history. It probably dates from the time when man first began to establish communal societies for his own self-protection; accordingly, laws became necessary to protect individuals against those who might exploit them. Obviously, penalties were necessary in order to enforce these laws. However, with the development of authoritarianism, the motives behind punishment changed; instead of being a means to protect the individual against those who violated laws, it became a method by which those in power enforced their demands upon their subjects.

The concepts of right and wrong also became vehicles for this control. Those in command were superior and therefore right; those whom they ruled were inferior and therefore wrong if they disagreed with the rulers. Punishment was the fate of those who disobeyed. This punishment was

[5] Spencer, *op. cit.*, p. 170.

necessarily retaliatory rather than corrective, deterring potential offenders. It was effective as long as society supported the power of the authorities. With the development of democracy and the breaking down of the distinction between superiors and inferiors the effectiveness of punishment vanishes.

At the present time, however, most adults who punish do not perceive that punishment today is still retaliatory rather than corrective in nature. A child who is beaten sees the punishing authority as trying to impose his will by brute force. Because the child resents the action and refuses to accept the authority as sacrosanct, he tries to find ways of defeating it. As a result, whatever corrective effort the adult had in mind is wasted. However, since punishment, like sin, is still so much a part of our tradition and upbringing, most of us still believe that children cannot learn to function without it; and we continue the old autocratic methods without being fully aware why they no longer work.

It is interesting to note, however, that in certain primitive cultures the concepts of reward and punishment were rarely utilized in rearing children. In her descriptions of a South Sea Island tribe, the Arapesh, Margaret Mead [6] shows how parents invoke what could be called a type of logical consequence. Children are not scolded, only helped if they get into difficulties. Little children are not taught to suppress anger, but to see that its expression harms no one but themselves. The girls get pretty grass skirts which would be ruined by the mud if they indulged in temper tantrums. They are taught to carry small bags on their heads by being "permitted," as a great favor, to carry their parents' posses-

[6] Margaret Mead, *From the South Seas,* New York, William Morrow & Company, 1949.

sions; to spill the contents would be a pity. As a result, the little girls appear to control their fits of rage and crying earlier than the boys.

In this tribe there is no distinction between the social status of children and of adults, so characteristic for civilized cultures. There is neither superiority in age nor in sex. Consequently, the terms grandfather, uncle, brother, or son are used interchangeably; the same person can be called by any one of these names, depending how one feels about him at the moment. Similarly, there is no status difference between men and women, little difference in their functions and activities. It seems to be more than coincidence that this tribe, which actually achieved a high degree of equality for all, does not use punishment.

THE CONCEPTS OF PIAGET

Unfortunately, the semantic confusion regarding the uses of punishment being retaliatory or corrective still clouds the issue even today. Jean Piaget, the French psychologist, who like Spencer takes issue with the value of arbitrary punishment, still tends to use the term in his applications, though, as he indicates, "punishment by reciprocity" seems to be closely related to logical consequences:

> There are, in the first place, what we shall call *expiatory punishments,* which seem to go hand in hand with constraints and the rules of authority. Take any given rule imposed upon the individual's mind from without and suppose the individual to have transgressed this rule. Independently even of the indignation and anger that will occur in the group or among those in authority, and will inevitably be visited on the transgressor, the only way of putting things right is to bring the individual back to his

duty by means of a sufficiently powerful method of co-
ercion and to bring home his guilt to him by means of a
painful punishment. Thus expiatory punishment has an
arbitrary character, arbitrary in the sense that, in linguistics,
the choice of a sign is arbitrary in relation to the thing
signified, that is to say, there is no relation between the
content of the guilty act and the nature of its punishment. . . .

In contrast, then, to expiatory punishment, *punishment by
reciprocity* is, to use the terminology of linguistics again,
necessarily "motivated"; misdeed and punishment, that is
to say, are related both in content and nature, not to speak
of the proportion kept between the gravity of one and the
rigour of the other.[7]

His terms "distributive" and "retributive" justice perhaps
more clearly define distinction:

Children who put retributive justice above distributive are
those who adopt the point of view of adult constraint, while
those who, in their relations with other children, or more
rarely, in their relations of mutual respect between themselves and adults, have learned better to understand psychological situations and to judge according to norms of a new
moral type.[8]

Though he seems clear on the differences between the
two types of adult behavior, Piaget's writings still seem to
suggest the need for very young children to be arbitrarily
punished, largely because to him they appear to understand it more readily than they did the democratic form
of correction.

[7] Jean Piaget, *The Moral Judgment of the Child*, New York, Har-
court, Brace & Company, 1932, pp. 203–204.
[8] *Ibid.*, p. 267.

ADLER'S VIEWS

Alfred Adler, somewhat earlier, had similarly pointed out the retaliatory intent of punishment and its ineffectiveness in deterring misbehaviors:

> Punishment is regarded by the child as confirmation of his feeling that he does not belong in the school. He will want to avoid school and look for a means of escape not by means of meeting the difficulty.[9]

Regarding the criminal:

> A criminal will interpret punishment only as a sign that society is against him as he has always thought. Punishment does not deter him. From the psychologist's standpoint, all harsh treatment in prison is a challenge, a trial of strength in the same way when criminals continually hear, "We must put an end to this crime wave." They take it as a challenge. They feel that society is daring them and continue all the more stubbornly.[10]

In the education of problem children, too, Adler felt that it was a major error to challenge them through punishment:

> We'll see who is stronger, we'll see who can hold out the longest. Their contact with society is sort of continuous warfare in which they are trying to gain the victory. If we take it in the same way ourselves we are only playing into their hands.[11]

At the same time Adler, in formulating what he called "the logic of communal living," [12] contended that children

[9] H. L. Ansbacher and R. R. Ansbacher, *The Individual Psychology of Alfred Adler*, New York, Basic Books, Inc., 1956, p. 401.

[10] *Ibid.*, p. 420.

[11] *Ibid.*

[12] Alfred Adler, *Understanding Human Nature*, New York, Greenberg Publ., 1927, p. 30.

must learn to deal with the consequences of their acts if they are to develop to maturity as healthy human beings.

CRITERIA DISTINGUISHING LOGICAL CONSEQUENCES FROM PUNISHMENT

Because of this semantic confusion it seems appropriate to define specifically and clearly the differences between logical consequences and punishment and to indicate the reasons why the former is more effective than the latter in helping children to develop in today's culture. The specific criteria distinguishing logical consequences from punishment are as follows:

1. *Logical Consequences Express the Reality of the Social Order, Not of the Person; Punishment, the Power of a Personal Authority.* This is perhaps one of the most important differences between the two approaches. The concept of the social order, when properly understood, can be most useful to the adult in helping the child to realize the results of his own actions. The social order represents the rules of living which all human beings must learn in order to function effectively within any given society. Many of these may be purely cultural in nature; others have a universality which transcends specific societies. For example, what we might call a purely cultural social order regarding etiquette in the United States dictates that when we are cutting a piece of meat, the fork is held in the left hand. It is then transferred to the right hand in order to pick up the piece of meat. In Europe the diner may safely keep the fork in the left hand while spearing meat. Violation of such a rule in our culture of the social order may bring embarrassment or humiliation to the violator. Though there are many

of these rules of a minor nature with wide variations in usage even among different social classes in this country and Europe, they still may be regarded as rules of the social order in that they are impersonal in nature and not merely proposed by the whim of an authority figure.

On the other hand, there are many more fundamental rules of the social order which transcend culture.[13] In all but a few primitive tribes stealing is a social transgression, the consequences of which result in relatively severe penalties, with the possible exception during wartime. Similarly, the crime of homicide usually merits the most severe penalties in all cultures, except during war. Although it is obvious that many social rules may be more harmful than beneficial to individuals in a given group, by and large they are designed to ensure safety and well-being. They represent the values established by a given society. It would obviously be possible to dispute any single rule as being truly representative of a social order; it is not the purpose here to enter such discussions but rather to show how the child may most efficiently learn to respect the established rules—those which are generally accepted by the members of his cultural group.

Perhaps one of the most universally accepted impersonal rules of the social order is the use of time. The concept of time appears to have been established primarily to ensure a more efficient coordination of activities. Accordingly, we wake up at certain times, we eat our meals, and are expected to arrive at work at certain hours; we make appointments for particular times, and so on. There are built-in consequences for most violations of these rules. Ordinarily,

[13] Adler considers the law of equality of all human beings as "one of the fundamental laws of human society"; *ibid.*, p. 225.

if a man is late to work, he may lose a certain portion of his pay, or, if he is late too often, he is discharged from his job. Parents usually fail to understand what a valuable ally time may be to them in teaching a child to learn to observe social rules. A child who has been out playing and comes home late for dinner is usually scolded—perhaps even spanked. A proper logical consequence in this instance would be for the mother to put the food on his plate on the table, and he could eat it at whatever time he arrived, providing the rest of the family had not finished their meal. At the conclusion of the meal, if the child had not yet arrived, the dishes would be cleared and he would get no dinner that day. Another example: A child who has failed to clean up his room at the proper time must delay his favorite television program until he has completed his task. A child who has dawdled in his work in class might then be required to complete the assignment during his recess time or after school. Thus, the social order in any culture represents a body of rules which operate on an impersonal level and must be learned in order for the child to function adequately.

2. *The Logical Consequence Is Logically Related to the Misbehavior; Punishment Rarely Is.* Punishment usually has no real connection with the misbehavior. It is usually arbitrarily imposed. In terms of application, this concept is most important. The child *must* see clearly the relationship between his act and the result of *his* own behavior rather than that of others. Otherwise, he will view the act as punishment rather than as a consequence. For example, two children are scuffling on the playground rather than participating in a group activity. The teacher summarily orders them to sit on the bench for the rest of the period. In most instances the children will be so antagonized by the command

of the teacher that they will fail to see the corrective intent behind it. It would be better if the teacher were to say, calmly, "I see that you do not want to play the game like the rest of the group; therefore, please sit on the bench until you feel you are ready to play properly." In this way the teacher effectively removes herself from the authority role by relating the result of their action to what they *are doing* and not on what they *have done,* and also by indicating to them that their return to the group is possible if they alter their behavior. Though there is obviously no guarantee that the children will accept this as purely corrective in all cases, the chances of being successful are far greater than by the former method.

3. *Logical Consequence Involves No Element of Moral Judgment; Punishment Inevitably Does.* Perhaps one of the few concepts on which most psychologists would agree is the one which recommends avoiding moral judgments in dealing with the child. Unfortunately, the traditional doctrine in the autocratic past has been to use moral judgment as a means of maintaining the power of an authority figure to effect a correction of misbehavior. As a result, all too often the transgression was against the authority rather than against the welfare of other human beings. The later Christian principles (after St. Augustine) also enunciated that any opposition to the established rules became a sin. Being good, therefore, meant conformity to the authoritarian rule. Because parents and teachers are inclined to follow tradition, their judgments about children tend to confirm this outmoded view: "If you agree with me you are good and therefore virtuous. If you disagree, you are bad and therefore sinful." Children, in conforming to this dictum, come to look upon themselves as good—therefore virtuous—if

they obey whatever rules are handed down to them, and bad—consequently sinful—if they do not. However, frequently they also see the injustice and authoritarian nature of these rules which are handed down by the adults, and are resentful that they cannot demand their legitimate rights without being considered sinful for violating the rules of the established order. Also, because the need of children to gain recognition is so much stronger a motive than their desire to conform, they are all too often burdened with guilt feelings because they violate these rules even though they believe them to be right. And because they have been taught to equate worth with being good, they often become convinced that they are "no good" because it is impossible not to violate rules at times. As a consequence, they turn more and more to the useless and destructive direction in life because here, at least, they gain recognition from adults, if not favorable attention.

The concept on which logical consequences are based, on the other hand, presupposes that the child is born neither good nor bad, nor does he develop arbitrarily in either direction. His acts may be judged good or bad by society; but this does not alter his essential value as a human being. His misbehaviors have to be recognized as mistakes rather than sins; and it is the responsibility of the adult to point this out without labeling the child as either good or bad. Punishment carries the connotation of sin. A child interprets his punishment to mean he has no value, or that at the least it implies that the parent or teacher has no faith in him as a worthwhile person. The logical consequence avoids making any judgment of this sort; it distinguishes between the deed and the doer. The child who experiences the unpleasant consequences of his act, in all likelihood, will view the act as something to be avoided in the future. Perhaps another important factor is that this relieves the child of the feeling that he is subject to the whim of an authority over which he has no control. A logical or natural consequence gives him the choice of deciding for *himself* whether or not he wants to repeat a given act.

4. *Logical Consequences Are Concerned Only With What Will Happen Now, Punishments With the Past.* Punishment is imposed on children for *past* transgressions. "You must pay for your crime" is the essence of a penal system. Again we see the relationship between the concept of sin and the old autocratic order. To atone for or expiate one's crime, one must do penance by serving X number of years in prison or pay a fine or both, as the case may be. The fallacies of this concept are becoming too painfully clear. There appears to be little constructive relationship between the number of years served and rehabilitation; with few exceptions, the more years a convict serves in prison, the *less* chance he would seem to have to avoid crime when he is released.

There is also another, even more important, consideration. When you have "paid" for your crime, ostensibly your debt to society is fulfilled; therefore, you are free to commit the same crime again, if you are again willing to "pay" for it. On the other hand, the consequences, natural and logical to the disturbance of order, are self-evident, and come into play *only as long as the child disregards order*. There is no element of "sin" or "penance" involved; as soon as the child learns that an unpleasant result will inevitably follow a given antisocial act, he will usually think twice before repeating the act. Thus it becomes order and reality itself, not the arbitrary power of the adult which brings about the unpleasant consequences. The parent or teacher can stand by as a friend, because the child does not feel personally defeated. Also the element of bribery (in the form of rewards for good behavior) or retaliation (punishment) can be avoided, as well.

5. *The Voice Is Friendly When Consequences Are Invoked; There Is Anger in Punishment, Either Open or Concealed.* The tone of voice is a very reliable gauge for human relationships. It indicates open or underlying attitudes. A critical and punitive voice can turn the best consequence into futile punishments. The greatest obstacle to the use of consequences occurs when they are actually designed as retaliation, as in the assumption "this will teach you a lesson." The application of consequences presupposes that the adult take a role as a friendly bystander. He can genuinely imply a regret, that under the given circumstances one cannot do anything else except let the child face the consequences of what he has done. A harsh tone belies any assumption of friendliness. It connotes demands, anger, pressure, or retaliation; they all are foreign to the application of logical consequences.

The friendliness has to be genuine, however. If the parents or teachers feel personally involved, threatened or defeated, they will be in no position to apply logical consequences. Then they are bound to fight it out, with the usual defeat which they can only barely mask by the use of punishment. Frustration and defeat are usually the result of pessimism and defeatism on the part of the adults who find themselves ineffective in controlling the child's behavior, because they do not have the means to exert an influence. The application of consequences provides them with effective means, provided they believe in their ability to become effective. Therefore, this is a vicious circle: If the adults feel personally involved, they deprive themselves of the benefit of consequences, which could give them an opportunity to disengage themselves. The technique of using consequences and personal disengagement depend on each other; one cannot take place without the other. And the tone of voice is the most reliable indicator of the personal involvement of the adult. One cannot conceal one's real attitude; the voice is a true barometer.

CONDITIONS UNDER WHICH LOGICAL CONSEQUENCES MAY BE UTILIZED

1. *The Use of Choice.* Choice is inherent in the nature of every logical consequence. The adult should always give the child a choice. The child should be asked to choose between behaving in the correct manner or continuing with his misbehavior. If he decides to continue it, then the consequence should immediately follow. An example furnished by an elementary school teacher aptly illustrates this point.

Example 1

A fourth-grade boy had been continuously in the habit of tipping his chair back while sitting in the classroom, despite the fact that he had indeed once fallen back on the floor. He insisted on continuing this attention-getting device. Finally, the teacher asked him whether he would prefer to lean back in his chair or sit like the rest of the children. The boy indicated that he would prefer to lean back in his chair. The teacher then put two books under the front legs of the chair so that the boy was leaning back in an uncomfortable, but not dangerous, position. The boy was then asked to maintain this position until he decided to sit properly. Before long he removed the books and no further episode of tipping his chair back occurred during the rest of the semester.

However, there are some examples of logical consequences where such a verbal choice is not feasible or even desirable. For example, the child who dawdles while dressing and then is subsequently late to school should obviously not be offered a verbal choice of taking his time or speeding up his dressing. In fact, the wise mother would even refrain from mentioning to the child that if he did not hurry he would be late for school. Obviously, after being late once or twice the choice would then be clear in the child's mind and no further suggestion needs to be made.

A common error often made by adults would be to offer the child his choice of "punishments" *after* he has misbehaved. The child will either select the one which is easiest for him, or refuse to take either alternative. The adult is thereupon forced into a position of providing an arbitrary punishment which only increases the conflict between himself and the child.

2. *Understanding the Goal of the Child.* As was indicated in Chapter 2, a correct understanding of the psychological goal of the child is vital to ensure the success of any corrective activities. Generally speaking, logical consequences are most effective when the goal is primarily attention-getting. In the case of power or revenge, the child is so busily engaged in either asserting his superiority over the adult or in getting even with him that he often does not care what results his actions incur. The more unpleasant the responses of the adults are, the better they fit in his scheme, in his desire to fight or to get even. Children in extreme states of emotional disturbance, anger, or hostility rarely perceive

consequences as the result of their acts but see them only as the punitive expression of a controlling or revengeful adult (which they frequently are). The most important rule to follow, if one wishes to use consequences in such cases, is to be sure that the consequences are not imposed by an adult, but are inherent in the situation. Such natural consequences which can take place without active interference by adults can be effective with children who are involved in a power contest or who seek revenge.

3. *The Situation of Danger.* It is interesting to note that critics of logical consequences always take pains to point out the specific examples where logical consequences obviously cannot be used. There are, of course, many such instances. A child cannot be permitted to run out in the street and be run over by a car to prove that automobiles are dangerous. There are many situations where simple prohibition is really the most effective answer, followed by removal of the child to a safer location, should he be unwilling to heed the warnings of the adult. A skilled adult can, however, often transform these situations into consequences through proper handling. A child who runs out into the street should be calmly and firmly placed either in the backyard so he cannot get out, or in a room where he is unable to leave; when he is ready to play in the front yard without running out in the street, he may then return. After a period of time the adult should then ask the child if he thinks he is ready. If the child says Yes he is then allowed to play outside until he attempts to run out in the street again. Then he is immediately returned to his place, each time required to stay longer. This episode rarely has to be repeated more than a few times in order for even a very young child to grasp the significance of his own actions and the consequences.

4. *When Consequences Fail.* In the subsequent chapters various types of consequences and their application will be discussed in detail, utilizing case studies as examples.

If, however, a consequence has been tried and has not been found to be effective, it is most important to analyze step-by-step each action in the situation to find out where the source of error might lie. Though often painful to the adult, writing down these steps can be an invaluable aid in objective analysis. Frequently the error will be found in some component of the adult's behavior—such as arbitrary command, an "I told you so!" attitude at the outcome, scoldings or reprimands tainting the consequence. After such an analysis, a suggested alternative often will be found that may prove successful.

It must be emphasized that despite the universality of applications suggested for the use of logical consequences, each application attempted involves elements which are unique in the relationship between any adult and child. All the correct steps must be taken to ensure the consequence being successful, but over the most important element, the adult has no control: *How* does *the child* view the situation? Success or failure depends as much upon this factor as any other. The adult can only apply his knowledge and understanding to the best of his ability and trust in the soundness of the technique to ensure the chances for success. In the beginning there may be many more failures than successes, as examples in the subsequent chapters will show. But time and experience in the application of logical consequences (with the resultant gain in understanding of children) will bring the successes to outnumber greatly the failures. Mistakes and failures will never be eliminated; but we feel the concept of logical consequences is so uniquely adapted to the needs of today's increasingly democratic culture that mistakes in its application are far less likely to be psychologically damaging to the child than those in the name of punishment. For this reason, the adult can use them with high hope and (most importantly) with a clear conscience.

To review:

LOGICAL CONSEQUENCES	PUNISHMENT
1. Expresses the reality of the social order, not the person.	Expresses the power of a personal authority.
2. Is intrinsically related to the misbehavior.	There is no logical, only an arbitrary, connection between misbehavior and consequences.
3. Involves no element of moral judgment.	Inevitably involves some moral judgment.
4. Is concerned only with what will happen now.	Deals with the past.

The user of logical consequences must understand that the technique is not applicable in all situations, and it is most successful in dealing with attention-getting misbehaviors. The adult must try to fathom the goal of the child before proceeding. Logical consequences should offer the child a clear and logical choice of behavior and results. The child must perceive that he has a choice and accept the relationship of his choice to what followed. Danger can be—and should be—avoided, and "firm but fair" is a good rule of thumb in application. The adult should try to be objective, but interested in the situation and its outcome, and must always remember that he is involved in a learning process —not in a judicial proceeding. Instead of being angry, he should be understanding and sympathetic.

PART II

Practical Examples

In the next four chapters a wide variety of both successful and unsuccessful attempts to apply natural or logical consequences are presented. Most of these are from reports submitted by teachers, counselors, and parents in classes and study groups. It has been found that though most of the users were provided with an orientation and appeared to understand most of the theoretical concepts involved in logical consequences, such as given in Chapters 3 and 4, their skills in practical situations proved to be quite another matter. However, their mistakes are extremely valuable because their analysis permits a clearer understanding of the pitfalls experienced by the average parent or teacher today. When they attempt to discipline children, they tend to scold, to threaten, to "explain," to make *sure* the children know what is right and wrong, to nag or admonish. This is still so much a part of our cultural pattern that a basic change in understanding as well as approach is needed before we can deal more effectively with our children.

For purposes of clarity, the chapters are divided into home and school situations, involving young children as well as adolescents.

CHAPTER 5

Home Situations Involving Young Children

The majority of the episodes presented here involve normal adult-child relationships in a typical American family. Although every family is unique and unlike any other, the episodes presented here may have occurred in many different homes, since most parents in our present cultural epoch behave alike and make similar mistakes.

In our approach to family counseling we have found it useful to examine what happens "during a typical day." Many times the parents recount events which they did not recognize as problems in need of correction. They often do not even realize their own mistaken involvement in problems because they considered those incidents as normal and unavoidable. It seems profitable to repeat this procedure by presenting the sequence of disturbances found in many families and to examine them in the light of possible consequences. It must be emphasized, however, that there are many other corrective approaches possible which may not fall within the province of this book.

BEING LATE FOR BREAKFAST

Example 2

The scene is a typical morning in the Jones's household. Mother and father and Tommy, age three and one half, are sitting at the breakfast table. But where is Ricky, age eight? The mother calls, "Ricky, come to breakfast!" No answer. A second and a third call produce the same result. Finally, mother gets up and goes into the other room. "Ricky, if you don't hurry up and get dressed, you're going to miss your bus for school." "I'll be there in a minute, Ma," Ricky protests. Mother returns to the table, obviously irritated by what has gone on. "I can't understand why I can never get that child to breakfast on time. Can't you do something about it, George?" "Ricky," the father calls in a loud peremptory voice, "If you're not here in one minute, you'll know the reason why." In a few moments Ricky appears, still half dressed. "But Mom, you and Tommy aren't dressed for breakfast, why should I be, as long as I get to school on time?" "That will be enough out of you, young man. Now sit down and eat your breakfast."

How often has this or a similar situation been repeated in the average American household? Though the dialogue may be different, the principles are the same: scolding, nagging, threatening, pleading, all these weapons used by parents are futile. Although Ricky usually succeeds in making the bus seconds before it arrives, he inevitably manages to involve his parents in a whole series of attention-getting maneuvers.

Here is an example of how a mother managed to solve a similar problem without need for the scoldings and the threats.

Example 3

Donald is awakened one and one-half hours before the school bus is due each morning. Still he appears at breakfast late and finishes eating only after much prodding, just as the horn sounds. After the mother and son had consulted a counselor, he came to the table to find it had been cleared. He was told that the bus would arrive in five minutes, and since he took so long to dress, there was no time to have breakfast. The second morning the same thing happened. The third morning he stated that he didn't care for breakfast anyway, although he was ready on time. So he decided not to sit down with the family. The fourth and fifth mornings Donald was at the table on time and ate a hearty breakfast. A two-year-old struggle seems to have been resolved.

What basically was the difference between the first and the second situation? As soon as the child becomes aware for sure that he will not be able to eat breakfast unless he arrives on time, the issue is closed.

AT THE TABLE

Example 4

Alice, four, is underweight and catches cold easily. Both mother and daddy are convinced that her health will improve with proper nourishment.

Alice sits in front of her plate, eating the first few bites with relish. She drinks a little milk, and as a conversation between mother and daddy starts, she gradually loses interest in her food. She leans her elbow on the table and supports her head on her hand. Listlessly, she pushes the food around on her plate. "Come on, darling," prompts daddy, "eat your good dinner." He speaks gently and lovingly. Alice smiles winsomely, puts her bite into her mouth, and holds it there. Daddy is again talking to mother. Alice's jaws move once or twice. "Come on, sweetheart. Chew it up." Mother interrupts her conversation with daddy. "You want to be a big healthy girl, don't you?" Alice chews vigorously. "That's my girl," daddy encourages. But as soon as mother and daddy talk again, Alice

stops eating. The whole meal is one of continually coax-
ing Alice to eat.[1]

It is obvious that Alice's lack of appetite has a purpose: to
keep her parents busy with her. The simplest way to "teach"
Alice to eat properly is to "let" her eat. If she refuses,
the parents should maintain a friendly attitude, abstain
from verbal reminders altogether, remove the unfinished
food from the table when everyone is finished, and allow the
girl to find out what happens. If she refuses to eat, she will
get hungry. And no food is offered until the next meal. If
Alice still dawdles, nothing is said. Friendliness prevails at
the table. If the child begins to play with food, it is casually
removed. There is no threat of punishment, and no bribe
of reward (with dessert or otherwise). And no complaint
of hunger an hour later must persuade mother to give milk,
cookies, or other food. Mother must allow Alice to be hungry, because this is the natural consequence of not eating.

Parents often feel no compunction upon inflicting pain
with spanking, and yet are horrified at the idea of the hunger
pain that the child may inflict upon himself in such a situation. One can understand the sense of deep responsibility
for providing food and for the child to get the proper nourishment. However, this concern of the parents in the child's
health and need for food actually brings the opposite result, namely, that the child will not eat, to keep parents busy
or to defeat them. Again, the problem could have been
easily solved, as in the following case.

Example 5

Henry was a very finicky eater. At breakfast he picked
at his food and complained because the cereal was not to

[1] Case taken from Rudolf Dreikurs and Vicki Soltz, *Children: The
Challenge,* New York, Duell, Sloan & Pearce, 1964, p. 77.

his liking. At lunch he ate only a peanut-butter-and-jelly sandwich, and at dinner, potatoes and dessert. Trying everything else, I finally hit upon the idea of merely putting the food provided on the table and taking it off whether he had finished or not. Though he complained bitterly the first two days, it was not long until he was eating most of the regular foods that were presented to him.

Another rather striking example of a similar situation was reported in one of our family-counseling sessions. The mother stated that the child wanted to eat only bread and milk. The suggestion was given to the mother to ask the child whether he would prefer to eat for a whole week only bread and milk or all the food that was provided. The child chose to eat bread and milk, and did not receive any other food even though he asked for it. Within four days the child wanted to eat everything that was served. After that the mother was not troubled with this problem and the child was less prone to do whatever he wanted. The dynamics behind this should be clear, though actually two factors are involved. First, the normal healthy child will rarely go one or two meals without food, if he knows that the choice is *his own* and that the mother really does not mind and considers it as *his* problem and not *hers*. The second point is that as soon as the child realizes that he can no longer involve a parent in attempts to force him to eat or to come to the table on time, he is then free to decide what he really wants.

Next we have an example of a good possibility for logical consequences which the mother spoiled in the crucial moment.

Example 6

Fred, age four, does not sit on his chair at the dinner table. He sits on his knees, off to one side, stands, walks around, and invariably spills something in the process. This is probably an attention-getting device since he cannot generally take part in the conversation at the table.

One day he again behaved in this way and I asked him whether he wanted to sit on his chair the right way or if he would rather not have the chair and stand up; so he moved his chair back and continued eating. Not more than five minutes went by before he asked to have his chair again. He was told that he could not have it back for this meal, but had to continue eating standing up since that was what he wanted. He cried a little, but continued eating, with the rest of us not paying any attention to the crying. At the next meal Fred asked if he could sit in his chair and was told that he could if he remembered that he had to sit quietly. A gentle reminder during that meal was enough to keep him in his seat. (We also included him in the conversation at the table.) His behavior seems generally improved, though occasional reminders are necessary. Part of the problem may involve the restlessness common at this age.

The choice of either sitting quietly or eating standing up was logical. But once a consequence has been established and accepted by the child, he should not need reminders. This makes it then arbitrary on the part of the parents whether they let the consequence take place or continue to remind him. One could either give the child a choice each time, or take the chair away and let him stand up as soon as he misbehaves. However, it would be better, and therefore preferable, to take his food away and ask him to leave the table as soon as he misbehaves again. Then it would be easier not to fall for the temptation of reminding again—and again. In either case the parents should extricate themselves from an emotional involvement; however, they have not done so. One can sense their pity with a child who, because of his age, is restless and "cannot" sit quietly.

BEING LATE TO SCHOOL

Problems are often easily solved when the mother decides that it is really the child's responsibility to solve them rather than hers.

Example 7

It was literally a Herculean effort for seven-year-old Jeanne's mother to get her off to school on time. One morning her dress was not properly ironed. On other occasions it was not really the one she wanted to wear that morning. Often the right garments were never around and the indulgent mother had to find them before the child would dress. Somehow Jeanne always got to school on time; but mother felt she was becoming a nervous wreck simply getting her to the point where she was ready to go to school. Shortly thereafter, the mother became ill and had to go to the hospital for an immediate operation. It was necessary for the father to leave for work before Jeanne and her twelve-year-old sister Sally left for school. Therefore a neighbor woman was asked to look after them and see that they were taken care of before and after school. Toward the end of the week Jeanne's mother remembered to ask the neighbor how she had fared in getting her to school. "Well, that was no problem," the woman replied, "when I saw what a fuss she was making, I just said, 'Well, you can go to school whenever you please.' The first two mornings she was late and after that there was no more problem." Taking her cue from the neighbor, Jeanne's mother made the same statement when she returned home and found to her great surprise that Jeanne was dressed and ready for school without any difficulty.

In this case it took an emergency to provide the proper type of logical consequence for Jeanne. However, most children will respond much more quickly to an outsider than to their own parents; someone outside the family does not take so personally what the child does, and therefore does not get as easily involved, either to give service or to enter in a power contest. Consequently, the child will be more cautious. At the same time, outsiders also generally treat children with more respect than do parents. There is more mutual respect and therefore more adherence to rules of order.

Example 8

Lunchtime was a daily hassle for mother, who was having trouble getting Carol, six, off on time to afternoon kindergarten. Then she heard about the system of applying logical consequences. Mother admitted that it was a matter of pride to he that Carol should be on time. It was hard for her to allow Carol to disgrace her by being late. However, one day she showed her daughter where the hands of the clock would be when it was time for her to leave for school, and then sat down to lunch with her. Carol dawdled, so when mother was finished, she left the table and sat in another room with a book. (No matter that the words went "in one eye and out the other"; she appeared to be absorbed in her own affairs.) Carol finally left for school a half hour late.

When she returned, mother casually discovered that nothing happened as a result of the tardiness. However, mother continued with the same procedure the next day. On the third day she wrote a note to the teacher asking for her cooperation. Carol was forty-five minutes late that day. When she came home she was crying because she had been late. "I'm sorry you were late, dear. Perhaps you can manage better tomorrow." From that day on, Carol watched the clock like a hawk, and mother ceased being concerned with getting her off to school on time.

One can assume that the first few times, when the child was still late for school, it was because of her realization that mother was still involved and watching what she was doing. If mother had completely withdrawn her involvement, she might not have needed to alert the teacher, asking her to take action. Then the example would have been really one of *natural* consequence, but mother's interference still made it a *logical* consequence.

HOUSECLEANING CHORES

Perhaps one of the most difficult areas of conflict between parents and children is in teaching children to take on the responsibilities of keeping their rooms clean and assuming a share in household chores. Children will learn to respect the rules of order only if they experience the discomfort that disorder will provide. All too often, they refuse to keep their rooms in order and to put their toys and clothes away as a means of rebelling against the parents who impose their demands on the child. Often the more fastidious the mother is, the more disorderly the child may be.

Here is an example which illustrates a rather typical mistaken approach a parent takes to the problem.

Example 9

Every week my daughter brings her gym clothes home to be washed and ironed, as it is required in her school. Instead of depositing them in the clothes hamper, she takes them into her room and leaves them wherever they happen to fall. The task then falls to me to hunt them up when I am ready to do the wash.

At first I mentioned to her that it would be much more convenient for me if she put her dirty clothes in the proper place. Then I asked her to put them in the clothes hamper. Thirdly, I threatened to leave them where they were and not to wash them at all. And finally, that is exactly what I did. This week when I went to do the family wash I did not take hers with me.

I do not know how effective this logical consequence will be since it was just employed this weekend. But I do feel that this is a true logical consequence since it was directly related to the misbehavior and it involved no element of moral judgment. The child had been forewarned of what I expected of her, and she knew the school rules that would be enforced with a demerit if she would not have her gym clothes washed and ironed.

The mother did not know how well her approach might work. But we can safely predict what will happen—it will not. How do we know? The mother is too much concerned, feels much too responsible for what will happen. She talks too much, she explains, she threatens. She gave herself away in the last sentence, "The child had been forewarned of what I expected of her." This formulation merely indicates a power conflict. The child knows what to expect and therefore will probably call her mother's bluff. She knows that mother is far less capable of holding out if she continues to ignore her responsibility. It is probable that the daughter could stand the demerits better than her mother could. The mother, in desperation, will continue to put on pressure, without much result, as it usually happens; in the end she will probably wash and iron regardless of what the daughter may or may not do with her gym clothes. Naturally, we cannot always be sure that this is what will happen. However, the pattern of the transaction between mother and daughter is so clear and so usual, and leading to the same continuation of pressure and counterpressure, that the probability of our guess being correct is very high. One can rarely succeed with logical consequences in a power contest, and the mother cannot apply consequences until she has extricated herself from her personal involvement.

However, if the child can see that his own freedom is threatened if disorder goes beyond reasonable bounds, he may be prompted to change his attitude, as in the following:

Example 10

> Susan, age ten, had many pretty dresses and liked to look nice. Her mother complained that she could not get Susan to keep her room neat or to look after her clothes. She would drop them on the floor and leave them there, expecting her mother to pick them up. Her mother was advised to tell Susan that her room and the care of her clothes were *her* responsibilities; and from this time on, any clothes not placed in the clothes hamper would not be washed and ironed. Susan continued to do as before; the mother stuck to her guns and stayed out of Susan's room. The day arrived when the girl did not have a clean dress for school. Mother expressed her regret, but did not see what she could do about it. Thereafter, the girl put her clothes in the hamper.

When the mother stopped telling the daughter what she should do, the girl decided what she *could* do—which changed the whole situation. Such a procedure obviously takes time and patience. With younger children sometimes a quicker method brings results. Toys that have been left lying around, particularly in the living room or the hallway, disappear. When the child complains that he cannot find them, the mother can say, "I'm sorry. I put them somewhere, but I don't remember right now," or "I couldn't clean up the room with them lying around the way they were." Eventually, of course, the mother "finds" the toys, but not until the child had experienced the discomfort of being without some of his favorite playthings for a period of time. In another method—though not for the fainthearted—the parent "accidentally" steps on one of the child's favorite toys which has been left around. Though seemingly unduly harsh and often financially expensive, this particular method may work where others have not.

With respect to disorder around the house, another, more dramatic, means has been suggested—only to be used rarely.

Example 11

A four-year-old girl had toys and clothes scattered all over the house. Whereupon the mother and father proceeded to leave all of their clothes and whatever work equipment or dishes or anything they had lying around wherever they had left them. The small apartment they lived in became so cluttered that there was not even room on the dining room table to have dinner. When the four-year-old became hungry and complained of not having dinner, the mother stated that she was also hungry but did not offer any solution to the problem. The child on her own went ahead and cleared a space on the table so that the family could eat. After that, her own room and the rest of the house was noticeably neater.

The importance, of course, in this episode, is the indication that all rules of order operate for the benefit of everyone. Often an imitation of the child's own misbehavior by the parent may be the most striking demonstration of the benefit of order.

LEAVING TOYS OUTSIDE

A similar problem is presented regarding outdoor toys not put away. (There is always the danger of these being stolen or lost which in itself may furnish an excellent consequence, if it occurs.) A good example of how this was handled, despite the usual parental attempts to correct misbehavior, is seen in the following:

Example 12

For several evenings my seven-year-old son had refused to put his toy wagon away in the shed provided for all outdoor wheel toys. He said that he was too tired. His brothers continued to put their bicycles in place after an occasional reminder. At first I bawled him out, reminding him of "rules"; but he began to exhibit "a violent passivity," crying out louder than I could yell. I calmed down, feeling ridiculous and waited for the next night. I was in luck as the natural consequence called rain became evident. I called the boy in and reminded him that his wagon was out in the rain away from the protection of the shed. I explained what would happen if he left it there. Vital parts would rust and he would have a lot of repair work and scrubbing to do before it could be used again. I told him that he still had time to put it away before it rained hard. I left the choice with him and waited. He said, "I don't think I will."

It rained and the wagon was untouched for more than a week. When he finally got around to it, it was in terrible shape. The boy was surprised and disappointed. At first he refused to touch it, then he kicked it, then the sidewalk parade of wheel toys began, manned by friends. The boy watched and quietly came into the house, took a soap pad, sponge, and rag and began removing the rust spots. It took an hour of elbow grease mingled with tears. After this he completed the job with wrench and pliers. He returned all the equipment and at six P.M. the wagon was in its place in the shed for the night. Since then, all it has taken is a gentle reminder to keep it that way.

This is an example where the mother almost succeeded in spoiling the consequence by her constant talk. It might have been much more effective if she had not indicated to the child in advance by the medium of an implied threat that if the wagon was left out, the rain might damage it. Confronted with this consequence, as he would have been, without all the talk and attention-getting, he might have put it away and would not have needed the "gentle reminders" that the mother apparently continued.

The following case demonstrates what might be considered to be a more effective means of handling the problem:

Example 13

The little boy had left his new bike out in front of his house all night. His mother told me that the reason she was upset by this act was because the bike could have been stolen, and because her little boy had not learned the value of such an expensive item. She wanted him to realize both. She told him he would have to put his bike in the garage and not ride it for a while until he was ready to put it in at night. After two days the boy was allowed to ride it again. The first time he again left it out, she put put it back in the garage for a longer period of time. Apparently after the second time this was effective because she heard him tell a friend later that he wouldn't do this again because he needed his bike.

OTHER HOUSEHOLD CHORES

An even more difficult problem is encountered when attempting to stimulate children to do chores about the house which do not concern their own rooms or their own possessions. Perhaps the most important single parental mistake is not so much attempting to enforce the rules regarding the chores but the autocratic manner in which this is demanded. The choice of chores is usually dictated by the whims of the parent without any regard for the children's rights or without reaching agreement. It is not surprising, therefore, that most children resent doing chores under pressure and do everything in their power to defeat the adults. The result generally is increasing conflict between parents and children, ending up with punitive action of the parents and retaliation on the part of the children. In this atmosphere utilization of logical consequences becomes virtually impossible; eventually different methods such as the following are needed.

THE FAMILY COUNCIL

The most important means by which parents can avoid such conflicts and implement consequences, not only with respect to household tasks but to all aspects of running the household, is the family council. It must be emphasized that the family council should not be utilized primarily for the purpose of assigning household chores; it is a forum where every member of the family has the opportunity to present his point of view, with regard to any of the functions of the household, as well as anything that affects his relationship to other members of the family. These discussions should be free and open, and every family member should be entitled to his objections and his suggestions. The meetings should be held at regular intervals, with a rotating chairman for each meeting. In this way the children do not feel that control of the meetings is the prerogative of the parents.

When parents are first confronted with the prospect of

such a type of meeting, particularly if they have more than two children, they become quite apprehensive about the possible consequences. On the surface, their fears tend to be concerned with mistaken judgments that the children might make. Generally, their fears are groundless, though there is inevitably a testing period in the beginning where the children try out their newfound power. Parents who are not easily frightened will welcome mistaken recommendations on the part of the children; then the children will be impressed with their faulty decisions and more ready to use better judgment, of which they are capable.

However, this is exactly the predicament in which many parents find themselves. They are neither courageous nor very bright when it comes to dealing effectively with children who use whatever intelligence they have to outsmart their parents. (The careful observer will notice that even retarded children are quite capable of outwitting their parents.) The family council provides one of the most effective means of teaching children the need to evaluate adequately the situation and the problems which come up.

The following two examples show first, a highly intelligent father who became dumbfounded and unable to use his head, and a mother who managed to let the children be confounded. There seems to be a law that only children have the right to be clever; it is our purpose to help parents to be a match for them, and the family council is one of the best opportunities for all to operate as equals.

Example 14

A scientist who impressed his family with his intellectual superiority presented a situation at the family-counciling session which he could not resolve. His three boys, ages ten, eight, and six, decided at a council meeting that the parents should buy a new house. The oldest offered $15 for this purpose, the second $10 and the youngest $5. What was he now supposed to do? He simply could not decide. He was convinced that the children did not know the price of the house.

To the counselor this situation posed no problem. First of all, he was sure that the children knew how much a house would cost. When they came for their interview they were asked about it, and the middle child guessed that such a house would probably cost about $35,000. The father didn't believe it when he was told afterward of their estimate, which was accurate. But still the question was: What shall I do now? It was suggested to him that he should be generous and offer $100 toward the purchase of the house and then tell the children to go and buy it. He simply did not have more cash available. Naturally, the children recognized the situation and made no further fuss.

Example 15

The second example concerns a mother with three teen-age girls. At an early family council meeting the girls announced that since they had the majority, they were going to set up their own rules about going out at night on dates. They were allowed to stay out as long as they pleased. They were not required to call in and inform their mother where they were or when they would be home. The mother argued against this position, but being somewhat more astute than the father in the last example, she wisely refrained from being arbitrary about the matter, although registering her vote as being against the proposal. Several days later she went to visit a friend, having notified no one but her husband. She stayed there all night, did not call in, and did not arrive home until about ten o'clock the next day. The girls quite agitatedly demanded to know where she had been and why she had not told them where she was going. Her statement was very calmly announced: "At the last family council meeting we voted to go out when we pleased, to

stay out as long as we pleased, and not notify anybody when
or where we went. After all, if this rule applies to you, it
applies to me as well." At the next family council meeting
the girls were quite willing to set up more sensible rules of
conduct with respect to dating.

Perhaps the greatest benefit of the family council in regard to household duties is the opportunity to outline all the
functions and responsibilities of various members of the
family that may not be apparent to the children. The duties
of the father are recognized as providing for the family's
livelihood as well as certain tasks which he has assumed
around the house. The mother has her well-defined obliga-
tions, and the children have to clean up their rooms, take
care of their possessions, and so forth. The remainder should
be listed and the children can be asked which ones they
choose to undertake. If the atmosphere is one of give-and-
take and not arbitrariness or demands, generally someone
can be found to undertake even the most unpleasant chores.
Experience has indicated that the performance of these tasks
is much more likely to be facilitated by agreement than by
arbitrary parental assignments. In subsequent meetings performance can be analyzed and the chores be changed around
to meet the choice of everyone.

It must be remembered, at the same time, even though
the family council helps children to feel a sense of responsibility regarding household duties, this is no guarantee that
they will be performed: Often logical consequences are necessary in order to ensure that the tasks are performed, as the
following case indicates.

Example 16

It was decided by our family that the process of clearing the
table after meals should be the responsibility of each mem-

ber of the family. This was to be accomplished by each one removing his own dishes. Our youngest son, Guy, age five, didn't always comply with this. When he left his dishes on the table, they were left there until the next meal. He was told then that he must either eat his next meal on them or put them away and secure new dishes in order to get his dinner. It was not long after that that he began to take his own dishes off at the proper time. (It probably took a little while because the parents still reminded him.)

Another example of dealing with dishes also suggests the values of a group rather than an individual decision.

Example 17

Delores, Jo Ann, and Barbara, ages ten, eleven, and twelve, agreed that each would do the dishes for one meal a day during the summer vacation. At first they did fine and rotated the breakfast, lunch, and dinner. Soon they began to put off doing the dishes longer and longer until the dishes from the last meal were not done when it was time for the next meal. We discussed the problem and decided that the person responsible for the previous meal's unwashed dishes must also take on the next meal's dishes, since it was impossible to tell which ones went with each meal. We could not use the natural consequences of not being able to cook the next meal when the dishes were dirty, as the girls knew full well that during the school year when I take the responsibility for the dishes, I usually do them only once a day. There has been no more dallying involving the dishwashing.

One wonders why the mother did not leave the responsibility for the girls during the school year.

In another instance parents, after having resorted to the usual scoldings and naggings, finally hit upon a method by which an outdoor chore could be accomplished.

Example 18

Jimmy and Stan, ages ten and thirteen, had the responsibility of keeping the lawn mowed. They kept putting the job off and we kept telling them to mow the lawn. It always was a battle to try to get them to do it—to get the lawn mowed and raked. Finally, we told them that if they mowed the lawn while it was still fairly short they wouldn't have to rake it. We succeeded in getting them to do the lawn a few times when it wasn't necessary to rake it. Then my husband and I decided not to say anything more about it. The boys put off the mowing until the grass was long and needed a great deal of raking again. After one experience of this, they now watched the grass closely and kept it short. They don't need to rake it anymore.

It was still the parents who made the decision as to what had to be done; it should have been decided in a family council.

Perhaps one of the most important rules in seeing that family chores are accomplished is indicating to the children that responsibilities around the house are not solely those of the parents. If the child fails to fulfill his part of the bargain to which he had voluntarily agreed, the parent may also fail to fulfill his share of the responsibility. If the children are too tired to do the dishes, then the parent cannot cook the next meal. If they are unwilling to hang their clothes up, then the clothes do not get washed and ironed. Generally, if this principle is adhered to, it does not take too long before the children begin to realize that a well-functioning household demands cooperation from all members; that their own welfare is enhanced by what they contribute as well as by what they receive. Again, instead of telling *them* what they should do, mother says what *she* will do or not do. This is the main distinction between autocratic demand and democratic leadership.

RETURNING FROM SCHOOL

Parents often suffer a great amount of anxiety when children fail to come home from school on time. Part of the problem may be caused by unreasonable demands. Overprotective mothers often attempt to enforce strict rules requiring the child to rush home immediately after school is finished. It is interesting that these rules are more often and more strictly enforced for girls than for boys. In the traditional masculine culture more freedom is allowed for boys than for girls. Yet some rules are needed for those children who habitually fail to inform parents if they want to stay at the playground or visit friends. Such neglect is usually followed by scolding and recriminations. Often a logical consequence can be simple and effective as the following example reveals.

Example 19

Charles, a first-grader, developed a bad habit of playing on the way home from school. His parents tried several methods to get him home on time. One day his father was to make a short trip to a nearby town; so he told Charles he could accompany him if he came straight home from school. Charles played on the way home and found father was gone. He was very hurt; but since then he has come home immediately after school.

Similar procedures are possible in many instances. If a child misses something he wants as a result of his own action, or if some benefits that he has expected are lost, this may be all that is necessary to convince him to change his behavior.

PLAYTIME

Example 20

> Jimmy, age eight, was playing in the back yard with a group of children. He was very bossy, not cooperating with the rest of the children. His mother watched the action for a few minutes and then told Jimmy if he couldn't get along with the children he could come indoors and play alone.

This seems to be a good example of a logical consequence. The child is not performing properly outside; therefore he cannot continue with the group. However, in reality it is not. Why? Actually, this is an unwarranted intrusion on the boy's prerogatives. Children need the experience of developing their own means of working or playing together in groups. If Jimmy's behavior is not acceptable to his playmates, they have many ways of indicating this. If his behavior is sufficiently uncooperative, the other children will refuse to play with him. The mother is depriving him of the opportunity to learn how to deal with other children, and this really makes it more difficult for him to learn the rules of the game. Only if there is evidence of possible physical harm to another child should the parent intervene in such situations.

FIGHTING

Example 21

> Four boys, ranging in age from four to twelve years, were having a fight before the television set in their playroom. They were screaming and hitting one another, were throwing pillows and magazines all over the room. Finally, mother entered the room. She started yelling at all four. First she asked, "Who started this?" After much confusion and loud accusation from all sides, mother threatened with "If you don't stop this once and for all, the television set

will be turned off." Then she walked out of the room. The children quietly watched the television for several minutes, but soon began fighting about the program. When their mother came back in the playroom, she threatened them again and left four quiet boys. At this point, as in the previous scene, the mother was threatening them with logical consequence. The third time the boys began to fight, mother turned off the television set and sent them to bed.

It is very difficult for parents to realize that such a form of interference merely results in increasing the frequency of the fighting. The great majority of children's fights are not for the purpose of solving the immediate grievance but to *solicit the parent's intervention.* If mother could not stand the noise that was being made, she could have turned off the television set and told the boys they could not see any program until they made up their minds and agreed on what they wanted to see. This pressure of reality is much more ef- fective than any word mother can say.

BEING LATE FOR SUPPER

Example 22

When our boy was eight years old and in the third grade, he began to come home late for supper almost every night of the week. My wife and I tried everything we knew to control this type of behavior. We tried: (1) *Logical ar- guments.* Food is better when it's warm and not overcooked. Mealtime is pleasant—we all get together. We must eat on time so the boy can have time to study afterward. All to no avail. We might as well have saved our breath. (2) *Punishment.* He was not allowed to play after school. This was partially successful because if he could not play, he was home on time. But sometimes he ignored this. (3) *Being put to bed without supper.* This was fine except my wife broke down and brought him a sandwich and milk after an hour or two. She did not want to see him go hungry to bed. His usual excuse was that someone didn't tell him what time it was. So we bought him a watch; we thought he had learned to tell time in the second grade; but he hadn't. His third-grade teacher informed us after we bought the watch that he couldn't tell time. My wife worked with him on the watch and reading it, but he either forgot to wear the watch or wasn't sure what time it was when he did wear it.

It seems apropriate here to analyze in detail these methods attempted by the parents. They provide—sadly enough —typical examples of the usual efforts by harassed parents to enforce compliance of their demands on unwilling children.

1. *Logical Arguments.* After the child has heard these logical arguments repeated a dozen times, whatever initial value they might have had is worn off. This is coupled with the fact that the parents completely misunderstand the aim of the child in being late, which is to gain attention and to force them into repeating the logical arguments they have attempted. The arguments are wise the first time they are stated. After that, repetition merely increases the reluctance of the child to carry out whatever demands they have made. Since he does not do what they have requested, the argument has obviously had little meaning and more effective measures need to be undertaken.

2. *Punishment.* As was indicated, such devices tend to work temporarily but fail ultimately because the child does not become willing to do what he should, only to give in to momentary pressure. At this point, he still has no tangible evidence that there is any particular value in getting home from school on time. In fact, from his view, most of the

benefits he is obtaining is derived from *not* getting home from school on time, attention, a sense of power, and so on.

3. *Being Put to Bed Without Supper.* In desperation, the child is put to bed without supper. But again, today's overprotective parents are so frightened by the probability of not "loving the child" enough that mother cannot bear to see him go to bed without food. It also offends her concept of a mother's responsibility. Therefore she weakens and the impact of the punishment is nullified. The average normal child is in no way physically injured by having to miss one or two, or even more, meals.

The child neatly circumvents the parental intentions by "forgetting" to look at his watch or by not being "able" to tell time correctly.

The parents continue their report; they began to get insight into the real nature of the problem. They finally attempted to look at the situation psychologically rather than on the basis of their anxieties and prejudice and traditions. Quoting the father again:

We finally decided that the way to combat it was to refuse to fix his dinner or do the dishes for him. His mother was concerned about his nutrition, but she finally agreed to let the balanced meals pass to gain the objective. On the next night that he was late, he was told to prepare his own meal and do the dinner dishes. My wife beforehand had agreed to sit in the living room and not move. My boy put on a sympathy-getting act that anyone would be proud of. He couldn't find anything to eat; there wasn't anything to eat. He cut himself; he moaned about how dirty the dishes were; he was finally allowed to go to bed when all the work was done. Each time after this his actions in the kitchen became less and less sympathy-arousing, and he started being on time more and more regularly. He still misses a meal now and then; but when he does, he prepares his own and cleans up his mess. Shortly after he learned the advantages of being on time for dinner he also learned to tell time very accurately.

The child was aware of this probably all along, but refused to let his parents know. This is a very good example of how parents find themselves struggling through the morass of their own outdated ideas and fears. They finally arrived at sensible and efficient solutions of their problem and then developed the courage to stick it through until the problem was solved. Unfortunately, this is seldom accomplished without some sort of help, either through a course for parents or counseling.

GETTING TO BED ON TIME

Other than who has priority over the television set, the major problem with which many parents are confronted is getting the younger children to bed on time. How late children should stay up without injury to their health seems to be a subject about which not much has been said, even by so-called experts in the field. As a result, a decision is usually arbitrarily made by the parents who often may try to get the children to bed early in order to have some time to themselves.

Children vary as greatly in their need for sleep as for food or any other vital commodity. One clue, of course, to this is in observing whether children tire easily or are inclined to take excessively long naps during the daytime. However, when the children are left to their own devices, without any parental attention, either in the evening or in the morning when they are tired, they usually pick their own hours for going to sleep and end up in bed much earlier than the parents expect. The following is an example of how a mother and father solved this problem and, at the same time, helped to assure that social order prevailed in the household.

Example 23

After making the children aware of the hierarchy of going to bed—the older the child is, the longer he can stay up— my husband and I decided that since it was summer, the children could all sleep late. We would leave it up to them when they would go to bed. The only stipulation was that they could not disturb anyone who wanted to sleep, and that my husband and I wanted to use the bathroom facilities from ten to eleven each night. This was agreed upon by all, and two of the children were finished with their baths before ten. But just as I was ready to go into the bath, Dale, age nine, dashed in and said he was ready to go into the bath, and go to bed. I said, "I'm sorry, Dale, but since I have to get up early in the morning you'll just have to wait until I'm finished." This meant that he had to sit and wait for quite a while until the bathroom was vacant. Since then he and the other children have made sure they were finished with their baths before ten o'clock.

For those parents who feel they must observe a specific routine for bedtime, the following presents a consequence which has been found effective in most situations.

Example 24

Mrs. Clark complained that it was difficult to get her daughter, age five, to go to bed when it was bedtime. Going to bed at eight o'clock, June made quite a commotion through making trips to the bathroom, requiring drinks and nosewipes, and so forth. By the time June gave up, it was nine o'clock, and Mrs. Clark was exhausted. She laughingly asked if I knew what to do since I was studying psychology. I suggested as a logical consequence to keep June up the next time until she was exhausted. Mrs. Clark was surprised but said she would try it. Next day, she called to tell me of the experiment. She was even more surprised than the day before; the method had worked. June's goal was to get more attention from her mother, which she succeeded in doing at first. Needless to say, June went to bed when told the following night.

It is not revealed here exactly how June's mother succeeded in keeping her up for that length of time. However, asking the child if he wants "to stay up as long as I do" is a challenge which few children can resist and which usually serves to keep them up long after the fun has disappeared.

There are, of course, many situations where logical consequences can be used at home but which are not part of the daily routine. There are a wide variety of conflicts where logical consequences may offer a solution.

CORRECT USE OF CLOTHING

Example 25

Guy, age four, consistently put his shoes on the wrong feet. This annoyed mother considerably. "For heaven's sake, Guy, when will you learn to put your shoes on right! Come here " Then mother sat him down and changed his shoes.

Mother is very wrong when she asks, "When will you learn . . ." Guy knows very well which foot is right for which shoe. Otherwise he would not be able to put it always on the wrong foot. That is all done for mother's attention and service. She can get herself and Guy out of this conflict situation merely by leaving him alone. If she does not interfere, Guy will experience the discomfort of wearing shoes on the wrong feet. She can also institute dressing lessons in the afternoon. Very soon the child gets fed up and decides that it is better to know how to get dressed.

Example 26

Joseph, age two, stepped in the mud puddle and got his shoes wet; he came into the house for dry clothes. When he asked to go out again, his shoes were not dry yet, and therefore he was unable to go outside. In a matter-of-fact way he was told by his mother, "I'm sorry, but your shoes are wet."

If more mothers would talk as little and act as much as much as this one did, parent-child relationships would be infinitely better. Another example of effective consequences:

Example 27

Sam, age six, refused to wear boots to school when it was raining. One day it was raining, which led to the usual fuss. I said that he could wear boots or stay home. I explained that if he remained home from school, it meant that he was sick and had to go to bed and stay there until well. Sam decided to stay home. He put on his pajamas and got into bed. Friends came after school to play and were told that Sam was sick and unable to play. The next morning Sam wore boots and went to school.

There might be some who would argue that this is an artificially contrived situation. This may be true to most adults, but children readily grasp the logic that they cannot stay home unless they are ill. If they are not literally sick, they must act as if they were sick to conform to school regulations. This quickly destroys any pleasure obtained from staying home. (The same procedure can be applied if parents are not quite sure whether an illness is real or pretended. In such cases the child should not be allowed to watch television or indulge in his usual pastimes. Even in cases of genuine illness it is not wise to overindulge the child lest he become convinced that illness brings a great deal of attention, sympathy, and special favors.)

Example 28

A mother left home for work before her seven-year-old daughter left for school. In this time interval the girl changed from her school shoes and put on her Sunday shoes. Ordinary punishment was being used with no results. When a logical consequence was suggested to the mother, she decided she had nothing to lose by trying it. The following is what happened:

The mother explained to her daughter that since shoes were expensive, she had to arrange when each person in the family would get new shoes. The brother was on the list next for black Sunday shoes, then the mother for a beige pair, and the girl next in June for a white pair. Mother told her daughter she could go ahead and wear her Sunday shoes if she wanted; but she could not hope for another pair before next June. If she spoiled the good ones, she would have no special shoes for parties or going away, but would have to wear whatever she had. The child proceeded to wear the Sunday shoes. When the first Sunday came, the mother casually mentioned that the shoes looked pretty bad for church and maybe the girl should take a brush and buff them up a bit. The girl did. The mother also casually mentioned that June was a long way off and shoes were so expensive. After this first Sunday, the girl never wore them to school again, and nothing was ever said about the whole matter.

An additional comment by the mother also illustrates a problem which many adults find difficult to grasp. The mother felt that applying the logical consequence in this way was quite a strain on herself, because it implied a hands-off attitude. She had a hard time restraining herself from jumping into the fire and using straight discipline. She thought that perhaps the ultimate consequence was too far removed from the present moment to have caused a solution of the problem, since the time element to a seven-year-old mind is vague. She recognized, however, that the element of withdrawing direct pressure perhaps eased the way for cooperation and made the consequences more effective.

Most parents greatly underestimate the intelligence of their children. Under autocratic family rule very young children were asked to perform tasks which would now be considered impossible to do. This comes partly from the autocratic assumption of superiority over their children on the part of most parents and, more important, from our present tendency to overprotect children, which prevents us from recognizing their abilities. Children by and large do not possess the ability to manipulate abstract concepts to the degree that adults do; nonetheless, in matters that directly affect themselves they have far better judgment and common sense than we are willing to ascribe to them.

In the previous example the mother may have been correct about the child's possible perception of events six months hence, but the child actually made a very quick connection between the embarrassment of wearing her Sunday shoes to church in a scuffed-up condition and not wearing them to school in the future.

HOMEWORK

Homework is obviously a problem not solely confined to elementary school children. When proper routines are set up early, much less difficulty is encountered with adolescents. It is questionable whether pressure on children with respect to school accomplishments, particularly grades, has any beneficial effect. The importance of establishing routines for doing homework at the proper time is indicated by the following example.

Example 29

Laura was told to practice spelling each night. This is relatively simple if done each evening at the same time; but she rarely wants to sit down and do the homework when she gets home from school. We discussed the situation when I found she was supposed to do the work. We had utilized a rather hit-or-miss approach to getting it done, and several times we forgot it entirely. Then we discussed the fact that this was an important part of her schoolwork, and set a time after dinner for homework. This leaves her time in which to play after school; and since we eat about 5:30, still gives her time for her work, bath, and to watch a TV program before her 7:30 bedtime. Both children enjoy watching 7 P.M. programs.

This particular misbehavior occurred on Thursday evening. (Her favorite programs were on Tuesday and Thursday.) Dinner was over and the table cleared by about 6:15 Laura was reminded of her work as I began the dishes. She decided she wouldn't do her homework. She sat at the table and dawdled without attempting to begin. Her pencil needed sharpening so she went to do that. Then she needed a drink of water because she was thirsty. This type of behavior went on until I had finished the kitchen and went into the living room to see the end of the news broadcast. At 7 P.M. her program began. She immediately wanted to come and watch. I explained that I was sorry but she would not be able to join us that evening. She first tried tears and then fussing, but finally did her work.

A similar occurrence happened on the following Tuesday. Thursday of that week at the dinner table she asked what day it was. I told her that it was Thursday. She said she was going to hurry and do her homework and take her bath so she could watch her program that night. We have had no further problem with the homework.

Although the action of not allowing the child to see the program was somewhat arbitrary, not strictly limited to the time required for her to do her spelling homework, it was still an effective action. Generally, it would have been better to state that the child may watch the program as soon as she has finished her work. Usually, children do not like to see only a portion of their favorite program. Consequently, it is not long before they learn to complete their tasks in order to be able to watch the entire program.

SHOWING OFF IN FRONT OF GUESTS

All too often in many homes parents greet the advent of guests with something akin to fear and trembling. "Just *what* will Jimmy do this time?" A simple, but effective, consequence for this type of behavior is furnished in the following example.

Example 30

Larry, six years of age, was a problem to his parents whenever they entertained friends. He actually would run around the front room, and boisterously and physically as well as verbally annoy the visitors. When anything was said to him in an attempt to correct his behavior, or quiet him down, he would retaliate with sarcasm. On one such occasion, Larry was sent to his room and was told that when he could conduct himself properly and show respect for other people's feelings, then he would be welcome to join the group again. He spent about thirty-five minutes in his room and returned to join the group once again. As a result, all, including Larry, spent an enjoyable afternoon without further incident.

The question is, of course, inevitably raised with respect to the above situation: What if the child refuses to stay in his room? If the parent has allowed a power struggle to reach the stage where such a possibility is likely, it may become necessary to have a baby-sitter to keep the child in his room. It is obviously important that children should be trained to respect others before they are exposed to guests. In some situations the parent may have to use force if necessary. If the child refuses to go to his room, he should be given the choice of going voluntarily or being taken. If he still refuses, he should be taken calmly and deliberately without any overt show of anger, and *without any talk*. Giving the child a choice is always more effective because it shows respect for the child's decision. It is more important to teach children proper behavior than to avoid embarrassing the guests who probably would be more than glad to support the mother in her action.

DANGEROUS SITUATIONS

There are, of course, many instances where the parent cannot allow the child to experience the natural consequences of his action as the result would be injurious to him. Parents seem at a loss on such occasions, as is illustrated here.

Example 31

Three-year-old Kathy refused to stay out of the street when she played in the yard. Mother had to watch her constantly, and bring her back into the yard. Scoldings and even spankings did no good.

The consequence of running in the street is naturally out of the question. One cannot let the child be hit by a car in order to let her experience the consequences. Before Kathy goes into the yard to play, mother can ask her whether she thinks she can stay there. And if she says Yes, mother merely watches. If Kathy wanders away, mother picks her up quietly but firmly and carries her into the house, telling her that when she feels ready to stay in the yard, she may try it again. As soon as Kathy expresses willingness to try again, she may go out. If she runs into the street again, she is brought back to the house, if necessary, for the rest of the day. If it happens again, Kathy may eventually have to stay in for a few days. But she always should get a new chance, when she is ready to stay in the yard.

Example 32

Johnny, age fourteen months, is an only child of a couple in their early thirties who worry constantly over small instances that are of very little danger to their son. It was a problem to keep him away from the clothes dryer when it was turned on. It gets quite hot to the touch, and Johnny used this to get attention when his mother was having a cup of coffee. As soon as he went near the clothes dryer, his mother leaped across the room, gathered him up, and held him in her lap. One day someone suggested that she let him touch the machine and see for himself that it was hot. It would not burn him, but would be uncomfortable. After patting it a few times, he said, "hot," and has not tried to go near it again when it was on. He not only quit using this to get attention but transferred his learning to other things that are hot, such as the stove when the oven is on.

The following example also shows how a mother effectively cured the child of the desire to play with matches without endangering himself or anyone else.

Example 33

Last week we had guests. There was a boy, Drake, nine, the same age as Jack. We noticed nothing while the people were here, since we were busy. Two days afterward, I found Jack and one of his friends down the street playing with matches. It seems that Drake had showed him what fun it was to dig a hole, put leaves, bits of paper, and debris in it and light it with a match. Further questioning revealed the boys had taken the matches from a drawer which I use for keeping them. They had played with fire during the weekend while Drake was there. They had such fun, they decided to do it again the day 'I found them. Since it was almost time for Jack's father to come home, I sent the other boy home and had Jack come in the house. After dinner we talked to Jack about fire, prevention of fire, the dangers involved, and so forth. We hoped that this would be sufficient, but we kept our eyes on his activities. We also talked to the other boy's mother, telling her what had happened.

For two days we observed nothing, then on Friday, Mrs. Kay called and said the boys were doing the same thing at her house and she just had to send Jack home. When he arrived, he came quietly into the house. I did not say anything to him about his activities, but waited for about half an hour, then asked him about it. Yes, they had played with fire again, yes he realized they shouldn't do it, and so on.

I asked him specifically why and he replied that it was lots of fun to see the fire. I then asked him if he would like to light lots of fires because I would let him do so if he desired. His response was enthusiastic. We decided that after dinner he would have a whole box of wooden matches and light them one at a time. But he must agree to use the whole box that evening. After supper we went to the store and purchased a new box of matches.

When we arrived home, Jack immediately sat down on the hearth and began lighting them. This was great sport for a time, but he soon began blowing the matches out sooner. In the beginning he would let them burn for a while. When he had used about three quarters of the matches, he said he was tired and wanted to stop. We reminded him that he had agreed to use the entire box of matches and had him continue. The whole process took about two hours. Besides the length of time it took, there was the rather unpleasant side effect of the sulfur fumes. When he was finished, he put his pajamas on and went to bed, since it was after nine.

The next evening we asked him if he would like to light a fire in the fireplace for us. My husband helped him lay the fire and then let him light it. He asked if he could be the official fire lighter for us. As far as I know, there has been no further repetition of playing with fire.

It should be noted that the parents helped the child to realize the constructive use of fire and allowed him to take a role in this responsibility. Thus the child learned to distinguish between proper and improper use of fire and to avoid using it for playing.

VERY SMALL CHILDREN

Perhaps one of the most difficult problems, at least one which parents mentioned most often, is in providing consequences for very small children who do not understand the meaning of words and who are dealing with such hazardous objects as electric outlets, hot stoves, and objects which can be pulled off tables and upset. Consequences can also help train children not to play with breakable furniture and objects used to decorate the home. Whenever the child touches the object, he is quietly but firmly taken away. The mother can point to a toy (*not* hand it to him) and say, "You can play with this." If the child persists, he should be placed in his playpen for a short time with the statement that "since you want to play with the wrong things, we have to put you in your playpen until you are ready."

After a while the parent should invite the child back into the room where objects are within reach. If he heads for them again, he should be returned to the playpen, but this time without words and for a longer period. After each repetition of the behavior, the time should be extended until the child responds. Few young children will persist for long, if mother *acts* quietly instead of talking. If the parent is consistent, even the child in a power struggle will realize that he cannot win.

Invariably, when such an approach is recommended, one or the other of the mothers will say, "But I want my child to *like* being in his playpen." He will accept it, if mother does not make much fuss about it. Care should be taken, however, not to overuse the playpen as a consequence, or for purposes of parental convenience, for that matter) in order to avoid the child's feeling that being in his playpen is tantamount to parental disapproval. Alternating use of the child's own room and the playpen may be a way of avoiding such an association.

FORGETFULNESS

Example 34

Ten-year-old Alfred frequently forgot to take his lunch to school. As soon as mother discovered the lunch, she would take it to school and make sure that it got to him. Every time this happened she bawled him out for his forgetfulness and reminded him how much it put her out to take his lunch to school. Alfred responded to these lectures with bad temper—and kept on forgetting his lunch.

Here mother has a wonderful opportunity to apply natural consequences. If the boy forgets his lunch, he would go hungry. He may be angry at mother for refusing to serve him; but that would not get him his lunch, particularly if there is no lunchroom in which to buy one or no money to do so. All mother has to do is to declare sincerely that she is sorry that he forgot it, but without personal involvement. If she were to add that this will teach him a lesson, she would turn the consequence into punishment. All this would presuppose that mother realizes that taking lunch to school is his responsibility, not hers.

AVOIDING "FORCING" THE CHILD

Example 35

Betty, age three, neglected to brush her teeth. In order to get the job done, mother had to go with her and force her each time. This quarrel upset both mother and Betty. Then mother thought of a consequence. She told Betty that she need not brush her teeth if she didn't want to. But since candy and sweets destroy unbrushed teeth, Betty could have no sweets. Thereafter, mother avoided any mention of teeth brushing. For a week Betty neither brushed her teeth nor had any sweets. The other children had candy and ice cream. One afternoon Betty announced that she wanted to brush her teeth and have some candy. "Not now, Betty, morning and evening are the proper times to brush teeth." The girl accepted this without complaint. That evening she brushed her teeth of her own accord.

"Forcing" the child probably meant the mother either brushed the child's teeth herself (which, in itself, would be difficult, if not impossible, if the child actively resisted) or stood over her while she did it, which actually meant the child was "forcing" the mother to stand over her and thereby give her one added attention she wanted.

ENFORCING PARENTAL RULES

Example 36

I have to work at night; therefore, we need rules for the children's behavior while I am asleep. I realize that it is tempting to disobey while they are on their own, but they have to learn to respect the rules for their safety and my rest.

Any statement that they "have to learn" precludes automatically the proper application of consequences. These words are dynamite; they indicate a power conflict and the search for a gimmick which will "make" the children behave and respect the rules.

One of the rules they had trouble keeping was: no friend or stranger is allowed in the house while I am sleeping. The children tried to have their friends in to play, naturally.

These rules were broken two or three times. Finally, I called my three children together and talked about allowances and what they stand for; it meant they were getting older and had shown responsibility and had earned the right to have some spending money that they could spend or save.

Learning to obey and respect rules is also a part of growing up. If they could not respect rules, it meant that they weren't old enough and consequently not old enough to handle an allowance. The next time they let a friend in while I slept, the allowance was automatically canceled for that week; and since then there has been no infraction of that rule.

Here we see a gallant effort of a mother to apply logical consequences. And one may be almost inclined to believe that she succeeded in doing so, particularly since her approach brought success. However, not all successful approaches are commendable. Withdrawal of privileges as a form of punishment can also get results. Yet, what punishment does is merely to create respect for the stronger power, in this case, for the person who holds the purse strings. Children who learn to respond to punishment usually need continued punishment for the most simple form of cooperation. The withdrawal of allowance is a powerful means; however, children are entitled to their allowance as part of their membership in the family. And financial penalties do not necessarily create respect for order, only respect for money.

What the mother did correctly was to try to establish a logical connection between allowance and refusal to bring their friends into the house while mother was asleep. This connection is obviously flimsy and contrived. There is certainly no connection between being old enough and not inviting friends.

In mother's defense, one must admit that logical consequences *are* sometimes contrived; but their logic must be acceptable to the children. In this example we do not know their reaction. The test would be whether their general acceptance of responsibility has been increased through mother's procedure, or whether they complied merely in this one area and got even with her in another.

Logical consequences are not the only method of correction, although perhaps the most effective, if properly applied. In many situations there may be no opportunity to arrange for them. This example may well be such a situation. Whatever the mother may do, it may turn out to be retaliation and, therefore, punishment. This is the inevitable consequence when mother has tried to put down the law:

"No friends in the house while I am asleep." There seems to be no preparation for this verdict, no consultation with the children. When mother acts as a despot, she usually gets what a despot deserves—rebellion.

Mother's need for sleep is a common problem for all members of the family. If mother had a good relationship with her children, there would be no problem. The children may recognize her need and respect it. If they do not, no gimmick will really help. Even if the children refrain from inviting friends, they could make enough noise to deprive mother of her needed rest. It takes more than one act, such as stopping a child's allowance—regardless of how well designed it may be—to win the cooperation of children. If mother has their cooperation, then many different ways of meeting her needs could be discovered.

Though this chapter has attempted to stress home situations largely appropriate to young children, it must be emphasized that many of the consequences presented may also be adapted to situations involving older children. The same may be said for home episodes involving secondary school children, though the analysis and interpretation of the dynamics involved may be different at times.

The parent or teacher reading this book should keep in mind that though many of these techniques have been repeatedly utilized successfully in different instances, each adult-child relationship is unique, and the methods must be adapted to the demands of each separate problem. The cases here are given to illustrate the general concept of logical consequences, not as prescriptions or panaceas for every problem.

CHAPTER 6

Elementary School Situations

As we explore various school conditions in regard to the possible use of logical consequences, it becomes apparent that the technique can be effective at all school-age levels and in a wide variety of situations. However, it seems useful to separate examples involving elementary-school children from those in junior and senior high school so that teachers as well as parents can see the application of the principles more readily in specific settings.

We will again proceed by examining a typical day, but in an elementary classroom, where the need and opportunities to use logical consequences may arise.

GETTING TO SCHOOL ON TIME

A universal complaint among teachers concerns students who arrive late. Usually this leads to a disruption in the class routines, and offers the student an opportunity to obtain a good deal of attention from the teacher until he gets properly seated, and has his assignments clear. After several such instances one teacher finally hit upon the way of solving the problem.

Example 37

Jim had been coming in late after recess. This happened several times, and caused him to miss the explanation of his seat work, which is given immediately following the recess period. Jim was told that it was not fair to the other children for the teacher to take time from the class to go over this work again just because he, Jimmy, wanted a little extra play time. The next time Jimmy came in late he was not given the explanation; therefore he could not do the work. When he asked what to do, he was told that he would be given the explanation as soon as the others were dismissed. Then he had to finish the work before he left. He has not been late since.

This is an excellent example of logical consequence (it was not a natural consequence, because the consequence was arranged by the teacher and not a direct outgrowth of the boy's transgression). The difference between this approach and punishment is quite clear. The teacher did not scold or admonish, but simply refused to give the boy special service during the class hour. Therefore he had to finish his work afterward, when the teacher had the time to explain the work to him. As he knew beforehand what would happen if he came in late, it was then up to him to decide what he preferred, to cut his play time or to finish his work later.

Use of the natural desire of children to participate in class activities, particularly when they are fun, also works quite well in providing a logical consequence for being late.

Example 38

Sherry, a sixth-grader, who never came to my class on time, was always from five to ten minutes late and had to have the work told to her separately or repeated. After about a week or so of this, I told her we would not stop the class and "clue her in" anymore but I hoped she could make the adjustment. Next day Sherry was again late and we were playing a new work type game when she came into the room. One of the students moved over for Sherry to sit down and said, "How is Sherry going to catch up with us?" I looked at Sherry and smiled; however, I made no answer to this statement. And Sherry remarked, "I'm late again, and so I guess I'll have to wait until some other time to learn the game." And looking at me, she asked if it would be okay if she read a book. I told her that it made no difference to me; what she did was her own problem. Sherry was seldom late after this little byplay.

It should be noted that the teacher did not hit upon this method until after "much needless attention-giving and repetition of the same offense." Unfortunately, unless the behavior of the child is understood, the teacher may not be successful in applying consequences. One must be aware of both the *purpose* of the child in attention-getting, as well as the way by which most teachers have trained themselves to respond.

ESTABLISHING CLASS ROUTINES AND RULES OF ORDER

It is a fairly traditional practice that the teacher sets up classroom routines and so-called rules of order the first day she meets the children. Frequently, the children enter the room to find the rules already written down on the board facing them; or they hold so-called discussions where, on command, the child immediately parrots out rules learned from previous classes. As a result of such procedures, not only do the children feel inhibited and uneasy about their relationships with the teacher, but the rules are regarded as impositions by adult authority and therefore are opposed with whatever appropriate weapons the pupils have at their command.

CLASSROOM GROUP DISCUSSIONS[1]

Classroom group discussions, if properly held, are invaluable in helping the children not only to understand the meaning and value of the rules, but also to implement their acceptance through logical cosequences. The following are some suggestions of how to introduce the topic of rules of order through classroom group discussions.

1. *Regular Weekly Discussion Periods.* A regular discussion period should be set aside each week, or more often if felt necessary, during which time children are encouraged to bring up whatever problems they may feel they wish to discuss.

2. *Don't Bring Up Rules of Order the First Day.* Until the children have had the opportunity to become properly acquainted with one another and with the group discussion procedure, possible topics like decorating the classroom, and planning activities for the week are more appropriate. The purpose is to help the children realize that the discussion group is a place where they can express themselves freely and where they can learn to understand the objectives and principles of discussions.

3. *Introduction of Rules of Order.* It generally is felt that the first rules of order to be introduced should be those about behavior outside the classroom. Gradually, the focus can be shifted to specific rules than affect students more directly, always avoiding emphasis on singling out any individual. However, even here there can be hazards if the teacher does not understand democratic procedures of maintaining order, as indicated in the following example.

[1] The authors are indebted to Bernice Grunwald for use of some of her material regarding classroom group discussions.

Example 39

> Safety on the playground has always been an important rule for me. Before I took my class of first-graders outdoors for recess at the beginning of the semester, I had a simple and vivid discussion on safety on the playground. We discussed the equipment the children could play on, the article or toys they could play with. After we discussed these points, we stressed not playing with sticks, glass, and not throwing stones. Then the children were asked to make a list of the rules they made and to decide what should be done if these rules were disobeyed. They decided that the "naughty child" should stay in the room and sit in his seat for one week while the others were outdoors playing. They all agreed to this, and we have followed through with this consequence, and the only accidents we have had were skinned knees and falling.[2]

At first glance it may appear that this is an example of democratic procedure and logical consequences. But it is not. The first doubt appeared when we heard "we discussed the equipment. . . ." One suspects that the teacher merely told the children what they could do and what not, instead of discussing it with them. One doubts that this was a democratic solicitation of opinions and conclusions reached. This suspicion is supported by the statement that "we"—meaning the teacher—stressed what should not be done. The final proof for the autocratic procedure disguised in a democratic pretense was the decision that the "naughty child" should stay in the room for one week. This is a typical punitive retaliation, first branding the violator of the rules as "naughty," and then determining the length of time he has to sit in order to make up for his transgression.

[2] Case taken from Rudolf Dreikurs, *Psychology in the Classroom,* New York, Harper & Brothers, 1957, p. 77.

One could easily use a similar procedure in applying logical consequences. First, one would have to refrain from name calling; second, the staying inside while the others were playing outdoors could be imposed *as long* as the child is not willing and ready to conform to the rules. It is a widespread assumption that young children have more or less to be told what to do and what is right and wrong. This assumption is true only for children who have refused to take on responsibility for themselves. Instead of falling for their "demand" to be told, a first-grade teacher has the responsibility of teaching them a truly democratic procedure, even if the results would not be as quick as those achieved through threatening with the big stick as this teacher did, forcing the child to "sit in his seat for one week." (One wonders how she achieved that without staying and supervising him during this period.)

Example 40

Due to the nature of my class (one which had been dealt with quite punitively by the previous teachers) I thought it wise to establish in a group discussion the specific problems that I felt necessary to discuss with the aim toward possibly helping them to set up logical consequences to deal with the problems. In order to get the children in the proper frame of mind, we took our reading period Friday and read as one group, Rudyard Kipling's "Law of the Jungle." We analyzed different laws at great length. The laws of the jungle were many and mighty; they were hard and exact but sound and just. "There was no one authority that made or enforced the laws of the jungle. Jungle's law was Nature's law," or said in another way, "The power of society or society's law."

After the reading the children appeared to have a better idea of the difference between actual law and punishment.

They also had a fairly clear understanding that antisocial acts carry penalties. I stated that we had a situation in our room that we might call an antisocial act and that the problems caused by it really affected all of them in the room either directly or indirectly.

I wanted to name a subject for discussion one afternoon. It illustrated an application of natural consequences in an area that was of interest to them and yet impersonal: The specific nature of the misbehavior of children arriving late to class. The group discussion brought out the following points: Arriving in class late does affect all the children in the room. (1) They are distracted from their work. (2) They are deprived of teacher's time when the teacher stops to give late arrivals directions or questions them.

Conclusion: The conclusion drawn by the group was that a person arriving late would not be admitted to the room, but would have to go and wait in the principal's office until the class had a regular break. Furthermore, since no one would have the time to explain the assignment or give the materials to them, their assignment missed would have to be done at home and returned the next day. After being approved by the students, this procedure also was cleared with the principal who readily agreed to support the idea.

For several days after the discussion regarding being late, everyone was on time. I was beginning to think that the problem had been corrected or that I would have to wait until after Christmas to finish—to find out whether or not there would be need to implement it again. The following Thursday, however, Jane, who previously had been one of the worst offenders, came into the room seven minutes late after having gone home for lunch. I had seen her come into the yard as we were lining up. She was walking directly up the walk toward our room but when she saw us going into the room she turned away and went toward the rest room. If she had continued up the walk, she would have arrived in the room as the last ones in the line were entering. I said nothing but followed the rest of the children into the room.

Seven minutes later Jane came strolling into the room. The class almost together said, "She is locked out. Jane, the train just left you." I said, "Jane, you may take your library book with you to read. I do not have time to go over your arithmetic assignment with you. We will have time to go over your assignment when we take a break at 2 o'clock." It was now 12:40. It was the last time Jane was late that semester.

Though in both of the situations mentioned above group pressure was also present in implementing enforcement of the rules, as a consequence even fairly punitive punishment set up by children in groups tends to be more readily acceptable than if the same rule were set up by the teacher. Moreover, requiring that the child wait until the class had a break was an ingenious means by which the social order was invoked to bring about a consequence.

USE OF GROUP CONSEQUENCES

One of the major handicaps and hazards facing the teacher in any classroom is inattentive students. When such a problem is widespread and it is impossible to single out a particular student or group of students who cause disturbance, the problem may be perhaps the students' boredom or lack of interest in the work. Outside factors such as extremes in weather, distractions, exciting recess or lunch periods, and so on, could also be responsible. Though the wise teacher will have developed ways and means of heading off such breakdowns in class behavior, there are inevitable situations which demand some sort of fairly impressive action. Then logical consequences for the whole class can be extremely effective at any grade level. One method has been found to be quite effective when there is considerable noise and disorder in the class. This should be used at a time when the teacher has been attempting to get some kind of learning across to the students. The class should be called to order and the teacher might say, "There has been so much noise here that I'm not sure whether you really got what I was attempting to put across, so let's take out our papers and have a little test." The teacher should then present the most difficult questions she can think of. When the papers are returned, there should be as many low marks as are possible to give, though the results are not placed in the grade book. In classes where most students are concerned about grades, this technique, if not utilized too often, can be highly effective.

In another instance, where the inattention was not quite as widespread, the consequence was applied as a result of the regular sequence of activities, though the students were advised as to what would happen if they failed to fulfill their responsibilities.

Example 41

My sixth-grade English class wanted to cover a unit in short stories by the method of panel discussion. I was willing, but as they are an excitable group, I wanted to give myself a lever over them. I told them that the continuance of the panel program would depend upon their behavior and how much they got out of it, to which they agreed. The arrangement we worked out was that each panel would be responsible for a different story. They would have to leave the class discussion to prepare some questions for homework.

They did a good job of preparing their own discussions; but I was aware they were not paying much attention to the ideas brought out by the other panels. I had warned them several times that they would be responsible for all the material presented, but they continued to be absorbed mainly in their own preparations. Came the test; naturally they found tremendous gaps in their knowledge. And for those who were not threatened by poor grades, there was the additional club of removing their exciting panel discussions.

We are now on our second short-story unit using discussions, and they practically discipline themselves as far as behavior is concerned. They also keep busy taking notes on the other discussions, an activity I had not suggested. If I had, I am sure they would have groaned.

Although the teacher was successful in applying consequences, there is an overtone of punitive retaliation. Repeated warnings were always unnecessary; they indicate the application of pressure and threats. The consequences apparently were accepted by the students, and therefore were effective. Individual inattentiveness may require different techniques, as the following example indicates.

Example 42

Lynn and Dawn were making an address book during the time set aside for library reading. I asked if they would rather do this than read their library books. They both said they would rather read. (The boys and girls in this class always choose the socially correct response.)

However, a few minutes later both the girls set aside their library books and were working on the address book again. I said, "I'm not sure that making address books is not more important to you, especially since you may wish to send holiday cards to the boys and girls at school. Let's look for some more suitable materials for you to use. Since you are taking time to make these books, I'm sure you want them to be very nice." The material we found was lined paper.

They set to work, and both girls at first were delighted

with the job. However, neither was finished in time for the next period which was social studies. Then they missed arithmetic. By the time the weekly spelling test was given, they still had a lot of work to do on the address books. Dawn got her spelling book so she could take the test. I told Dawn that this was her day for fixing her address book and she needn't bother with the test. Dawn began to cry. Immediately Lynn was in tears. They worked on the address books with noted disinterest. At lunchtime both girls came to see me and said they didn't want to work on their books any longer. They also requested that I give them their spelling test after school. The procedure was quite successful.

As will happen in some instances, children may give the socially correct answer in the hope that they can disregard it later and that the teacher will not notice it. This was apparently what the two girls did. However, the teacher let them choose what they really wanted, and then wisely allowed them to go ahead with it in order to invoke the consequence.

FOLLOWING INSTRUCTIONS

Another quite persistent problem which plagues most teachers is the student who continually misunderstands or does not hear the assignment. In a great many instances this is an attention-getting device for which the teacher usually falls. The following example reported by a student teacher illustrates how the problem was solved very quickly.

Example 43

A fifth-grade class had a problem of students who couldn't seem to understand any instructions. No matter how clearly and slowly the directions were given, the same four or five children would always say they didn't understand. The teacher would then have to repeat the instructions as many as ten times for them. Other teachers had also had the same difficulty with this group. The process was holding back the rest of the class.

The children in question were not slow learners, but had a fairly consistent record of good grades. On a particular day when it was necessary to explain the directions for an art project, before I began, the supervising teacher said to the children, "Mr. Jones can spend only a few minutes with us today as he has to leave for a meeting. He will give the instructions two times and then he has to leave."

I gave the directions; and as could be expected, when I finished for the second time, the five students in question immediately started asking me to show them again because they didn't understand. The supervising teacher indicated that they had gotten the instructions and told them to go to work. When it came time to grade the project, the students who had previously not understood the instructions had done the projects without a single mistake. This was the last time this type of behavior was exhibited by them in my class.

Actually, there may be instances where failure to understand instructions may be the teacher's responsibility as much as the students'. One particularly useful rule which is applicable to all grade levels, except first and second, is always to have instructions for a particular assignment either mimeographed or written on the blackboard in clear, easy-to-read style. Then if the child asks further questions, as if the assignment were not understood, the teacher merely has to point to the board or to the newsprint and say, "See for yourself." In such a way a great deal of unnecessary talk and potential attention-getting is avoided.

THE SHOW-OFF

Perhaps the most universal disruption of classroom routines is through the antics of the show-off. His repertoire of misbehavior is literally endless. It is often said that because of him more teachers leave the profession than from any other cause. As it is obviously impossible to deal with all the various forms of this behavior pattern and their possible consequences that might be involved, only those that appear to be the most common are being selected.

Excessive Talking

Excessive talking, either by interrupting or by carrying on private conversations, is probably the most common form of showing-off. Many a teacher fails to realize that such behavior is directed to her either to get her attention or to challenge her leadership. The following instance was reported:

Example 44

Beth always had the same troubles. She used any method available to call attention to herself. Her mouth was always open; she was always talking to someone and everyone in sight, and that at a very loud pitch. She constantly was disturbing her neighbors and seemed to be unable to concentrate on her work. When the report cards came out she proceeded, after she had surveyed her card, to yell out to her classmates what grades she had received.

I called her up to my desk. She came up quite loudly. I told her that it was not polite to disturb other people in the class, and if she wanted to belong and be included she should be a little more subtle. She was very calm and seemed to understand what I meant.

The next day when she came into class she took her seat quietly and didn't talk out loud. I believe this was the logical consequence because I talked to her and didn't punish her for action.

This example shows how difficult it is for some teachers to grasp the meaning of logical consequences. Merely refraining from punishing does not constitute learning through consequences. All the teacher was doing was preaching and admonishing. That the girl was quiet the next day does not prove that she has changed her behavior. The teacher will have to do much more if she wants to influence the girl. What could be done?

First of all, influencing such a child's behavior usually requires helping her understand what she is doing. In this case, demanding constant attention, being the center. One can be sure that Beth was not the only child with this intention. Therefore one needs group discussions to help children understand themselves and others and help them to correct their behavior. But is there a possibility of applying logical consequences? One could make an agreement with her and with the class that whenever Beth disturbs the class, the class procedure would stop until she quiets down. If she is loud while the report cards are given out, the teacher can stop the procedure again until everything is again quiet. The refusal of the teacher to continue whatever she is doing when the class is noisy is one of the best and simplest forms of logical consequences. Her quietness speaks much louder than anything she can say. Only too often does a teacher add her noise to that of the class, in the vain hope that this will make the class quiet. On the other hand, a teacher who is hoarse, may find to her amazement that her students have become unusually quiet.

Private conversations can sometimes be ignored, unless they distract the other children or result in the participants missing too much of the work. For this type of behavior the following was found to be quite effective.

Example 45

When we were reciting our lesson in my fourth-grade class, Nancy and Viola, who were sitting close together, were having a private conversation, using sign language. I tried to attract their attention by simply looking in their direction; but they were so busy they didn't see me. Finally, I said, "Nancy and Viola, you seem to have something important to say to each other, something that can't wait until class is dismissed. You two may go out in the hall and tell each other what you want to say—and when you are through you may come back."

As they started out, Viola said, "I wasn't talking." I said, "I know you weren't, but your hands were."

The two children went out, but returned in a few minutes and joined our oral discussion. After school Viola came to me and asked me if I would change her seat the next day. I did.

In this example the teacher did not talk unnecessarily. She first tried to stop the girls by merely looking at them. It is probably that the girls really did not notice this at first, and the teacher could have stopped them perhaps by merely calling their names and looking without saying anything. This might have been sufficient; if the girls continued, then a more impressive action would have been necessary. The teacher succeeded in making the logic of the consequence clear to the children. The smooth and calm handling of the disturbance had a deep effect.

The next example, reporting a similar problem, raises

some interesting questions regarding our change in attitudes about how to deal with childhood misbehavior.

Example 46

> I was in a first-grade classroom as a student observer. The teacher had to leave the room for a few minutes and asked if I would call the roll and get the class started. While I was calling the roll, the children were supposed to be sitting quietly as their teacher had instructed them to do. They were all quiet except for one boy and girl. These two were discussing the next day's May Day dance and going through the motions of the dance they were to do with their hands. The other children became increasingly distracted. Finally, I asked the two to come up in front of the room and show the class how their part in the dance was to be done. They come, but they only stood quietly. I asked, "Don't you want to show the class how to do your dance?" The girl answered, "No, I'm embarrassed." I asked them if they would like to return to their places and sit quietly, and they replied that they would. They were quiet for the rest of the time until the teacher returned.

Such a procedure might be considered by some, particularly those who support the Freudian doctrines regarding behavior, as humiliating. In the old, autocratic classrooms children were humiliated by being exposed and belittled in front of the class, being labeled stupid, having to wear the dunce's cap, or being termed "lazy." Such public rebuking was thought to be morally sound and to extoll the virtues of being right against the sin of being wrong. The use of moral condemnation was designed to be humiliating; it deliberately fostered feelings of guilt and shame. Today it no longer brings the desired results. In the above incident, no attempt was made to judge whether their behavior was good or bad, right or wrong. Though the children were obviously embarrassed, it was a result of their own action and not a result of any arbitrary judgment by the teacher. She did not preach, but acted quietly and effectively.

Often the misbehaviors of a child who plays a leadership role in the class may incite misbehavior and disruption of other students and ultimately of the whole class itself. The teacher must be constantly on the alert to spot such disturbances and head them off before they become contagious. The following is an example of how this was attempted:

Example 47

John was the undisputed leader of the second-grade class. He was a nice boy, good in his homework and athletics; all the girls and boys in the class looked up to him. So when John started showing off in front of the class by talking out of turn, squirming, and so on, they responded. The teacher knew that she would have trouble with the whole class unless she stopped John. She knew that he as well as the rest of the class would have to be taken by surprise. One day John was talking out of turn and disrupting the class again. The teacher stopped, turned to John and said, "You have been purposely disrupting the class with your talking. I don't believe you are yet ready to be in the second grade. You should go back to the kindergarten and think about how a second-grader should act." All the other children were as surprised as John. The tears welled in his eyes as the teacher marched him to the kindergarten room. About an hour later John came sheepishly back to the second-grade classroom. He had learned his lesson. He was now ready to be a second-grader. Ever since that time he has been a fine leader and pupil and has not disrupted the class once.

The teacher was arbitrary in the way she handled the situation even though her corrective effort obviously worked. She could have said to John, "I'm not really quite sure whether you are ready to continue in second grade because of all the disruptions you have been causing. If it is difficult for you to behave differently, it might be better for you to try and go back to kindergarten for a while and see whether there is a difference between the way second-graders act and the way kindergartners act." She also should have indicated to him that when he was ready to come back to the second grade, he could. In this way she would have avoided the pitfalls of punitive retaliations.

The following is another example where the teacher spoiled the consequence by an arbitrary action:

Example 48

Sandy's goal was simply to attract attention. I spoke to the child about being out of his seat. This did not seem to solve the problem. Sandy remained in his seat only for several days. The next time I caught him out of his seat I said, "Since you prefer to be out of your seat, you may stand at attention at your desk for the remainder of the period. Since the period is almost over, you can stand by your desk tomorrow."

In this case standing "at attention" by his seat has obvious military implications and carrying it over for the next day is certainly against the principle of applying logical consequence. The child should have been given a choice the next day. A far better method of handling such a misbehavior might be the following:

Example 49

A few weeks ago one of the boys in our classroom was constantly getting out of his seat, leaning on his desk, and doing his work from a half-standing position. I finally asked him whether he would rather stand or sit while doing his work. It made no difference to me which way he preferred. The boy stated that he would prefer standing. I explained to him he would then no longer need his seat and we could therefore take the chair out of the room, which we did, allowing the boy to stand up for the rest of the day. The following day, at the beginning of the period, I asked the boy whether he would like standing or sitting. This time he preferred sitting, and we no longer had any dfficulty with him about his half-standing position.

In this case the boy was offered his choice, and having taken the decision to stand, he therefore had to suffer the consequences of his decision.

Chair-tipping

One of the favorite tactics of children who show off is leaning back in their chairs. The following example of a natural consequence, but one which could have been avoided, is taken from one of our earlier writings and tells what happened in this situation: [8]

Example 50

Ernie is a first-grader who is happiest when he is the center of attention. From the first day of school, he rocked back and forth in his chair usually catching himself just before he tipped back far enough to fall. His teacher pointed out the hazards of this activity, but Ernie continued rocking. One day there was a mighty crash; Ernie had rocked too far. He got up, rubbed himself, and sat down quietly. The children paid no attention and the teacher continued with the reading group. He appeared not to notice. I believe this is a situation of natural consequence because Ernie suffered some results of his behavior so he did not gain any desired attention from the group. At present, Ernie uses the chair to sit on rather than as a piece of gymnastic equipment.

[8] *Ibid.,* p. 78.

Letting the child experience the consequence was truly an application of natural consequences, since they occurred without the adult's intervention. It was significant that no attention was paid to the event, which would have provided Ernie with a satisfaction for his misdeed, surpassing the distress of the consequence. And yet the teacher really failed in her purpose. There was no reason for letting the child during all this time continue with his disturbing behavior. Pointing out its hazards is both unnecessary and preachy. The child knows exactly what would happen. But he preferred the danger of a fall since it kept the teacher's eye focused on him, and showed her his determination to continue what he wanted to do. In other words, the situation before the final fall was not handled properly and efficiently. It is obviously not advisable, particularly in the classroom, to expose the child to an accident in which he may get hurt. He might not mind this as much as the teacher and the parents would.

Here is another example of a teacher who was "desperate" to provide a remedy and succeeded only in being punitive rather than corrective:

Example 51

Jimmy was a five-year-old kindergartner. He enjoyed sitting on his chair using only two legs instead of four. Since the classroom floor was highly waxed, the two chair legs would slip from under him and he would crash to the floor, sometimes hurting himself. He enjoyed having the children laugh at him, causing a disturbance, and irritating me. Several reminders did not help the situation and I was afraid that some day he might suffer from a severe neck or head injury if he were to hit the desk behind him. So I decided to take the chair away from him and have him kneel for a while, in order for him to do his seat work. When he tried to stand or sit, I would not allow it; so this proved uncomfortable and painful for him. When he was ready for the chair, he was welcome to it. Each time it happened, I extended the time he would have to spend on his knees. Seeing that the other children did not join him in his antics and that I did not sympathize with his painful knees, it stopped after a few times. If I were to be faced with this situation again, I would not talk as much as I probably did in warnings and in the actual taking away of the chair.

In this instance the teacher, in making the boy kneel, provided an arbitrary demand that was not related to the misbehavior.

But what could the teacher have done? There are many things. First, she might have discussed the matter with the children and they could have decided together what to do about it. This can be effective even in kindergarten. Possibly an appropriate logical consequence in this instance also might have been to put books under the boy's chair, as mentioned in Chapter 4 (Example 1, p. 78), or merely to have deprived him of a chair for the rest of the hour—but as soon as he starts rocking and without words, without preaching, advising, or scolding. Or he can be excused from the class until he is ready to sit down quietly.

All these, of course, should not be arbitrary decisions of the teacher, but possible solutions arrived at in a class discussion in which the child has the right to participate. One may even ask him directly what he thinks should be done in such a situation. More important than all these manipulations is a frank discussion of the problem which these children probably share with many others, namely, the demand for constant attention. Though they may stop rocking the chair, this seldom relieves the constant bids for attention. This is really the major problem.

The Child Who Interrupts

A child who is constantly interrupting whenever the teacher is attempting to put over a point with others in the class, or when another child is talking, also presents a problem that is difficult to solve. This was effectively dealt with as follows:

Example 52

Constant interruption at the most inconvenient time is a continual problem with Sam. He interrupts class discussions without raising his hand, makes unnecessary trips to my desk during seat work, barges into conversations uninvited, and disrupts a great many pupil-teacher conferences with insignificant, irrelevant comments and questions. This problem has caused me much consternation and taxed the patience of the class.

During one particular social studies discussion he made himself particularly offensive with unsolicited interruptions. After my repeated requests that he raise his hand, wait his turn, and other constructive suggestions failed, I reprimanded him sternly and demanded that he raise his hand. He slouched and remained still for a few minutes, then raised his hand. After comments from one or two others, I called on him. After he had uttered no more than four or five words, I began talking to some other student in the class. He stopped talking and so did I. He started talking again, this time about something completely foreign to the subject at hand. The same sequence was repeated. He finally gave up the attempt to deliver his comment. After a very brief lull, he gaped at me and with his voice reflecting distress reminded me that I had interrupted him three times, and that this was a rude thing to do. I acknowledged the fact that I had interrupted him and that it was rude but stated that this was exactly what he himself had done just prior to the interruption of which I was guilty.

I said that I didn't think he was concerned about such rudeness so it wouldn't matter if I interrupted him. I continued by saying I was glad he felt this way because now he knows exactly how I feel and how others feel when they are interrupted and not allowed to finish what they are saying.

I feel that Sam learned a lesson with this new experience. His interruptions during discussions have greatly decreased. Even when he unwittingly errs, he realizes his misdeed and in his peculiar way acknowledges it. He still has a million things to tell me, seemingly a million times a day. But the basic change in his behavior is that he now awaits his turn even if it takes ten minutes.

Although it was not necessary for the teacher to go into a moral discourse on the relative merits or demerits of interrupting, which was something the child was well aware of, it was useful to point out that the tables could be turned. Often the discomfort of being inconvenienced by the same kind of behavior that the child himself has been demonstrating may be the only way to convince him of the need to refrain from such behavior in the future.

Children Not Remaining in Their Seats

Example 53

Barry had been getting up from his seat several times to go over and talk to various other children during reading, science, and social studies. He did not whisper to the others, but talked in a normal voice which disturbed the class. I consider his behavior an AGM [Attention-Getting Mechanism]. From what the mother told me about his behavior at home, he could also be in a power conflict, although his classroom behavior did not suggest this.

After the fourth time on one day that Barry got up, I went over to his seat and told him quietly that I would like to see him at my desk before the class went to lunch. At noon he came to my desk and I said that he seemed to be having difficulty staying in his seat. He replied that he got up just because he "felt like it and wanted to check on what the other boys were doing." I mentioned that he might be getting up because he wanted the other boys' attention or perhaps mine. At this, he just shrugged his shoulders but didn't say anything. Then I said, "Barry, I have got an idea that may help you overcome this problem. I would like to give you a choice between staying in your seat, or getting up every fifteen minutes, for the entire day, and walking to the rear door and back to your seat."

He said he wanted to stay in his seat. I said all right, but if it happened again he would take the other alternative. He agreed to this.

Two days went by and nothing happened. About nine thirty the third morning he got out of his seat and went over to another boy's seat and they began giggling. I caught Barry's eye and pointed to the clock. He caught on right away and walked to the door and back to his seat. After recess he continued this until noon. After lunch I had to remind him once, and he continued this until school was out for the day. On the fourth day he came up and asked me if he would have to walk again as he had before. I said, "Only if you get out of your seat again." So far he has not done so.

This interesting example raises a number of important questions. First, was the teacher's diagnosis of attention-getting correct? It seems it was, otherwise the boy might have shown more defiance when approached. But was she wise in confronting him with his goals in the way she did? Partly yes, partly not. There is a definite sequence of three questions which seems to be required in giving the child insight into his goal and evoking the "Recognition Reflex." [4]

___

[4] For further description of this concept see *ibid.*, p. 47.

She made the first step correctly by asking him why he got up, and as is usually the case, the child gave some rationalizations, because no child knows the real purpose of his behavior. But then the teacher did not follow through with the next steps. She should have first asked him whether he would like to know what she thought was the reason. Then she should have expressed her opinion in the form of a question. "Could it be that you did this because you wanted our attention?" The boy would then have had to think it over, and if the guess was right, he probably would have responded with the Recognition Reflex. As it was, he merely shrugged his shoulders to the teacher's statement. But in general the teacher moved in the right direction in discussing the situation with him.

Even more interesting is the question: Did the teacher really apply logical consequences? She almost did, but she did not quite succeed. In order for consequence to be logical and not arbitrary, the logic must be made clear to the child. As she proceeded, she gave the child two choices; but she was arbitrary in making one as definite as she did, that is, walk every fifteen minutes for the whole day. She could have indicated a possible logical connection between the two choices. She could have pointed out to Barry that on some days it seems to be difficult for him to stay in his seat. Therefore, whenever he felt like getting up, she offered him the choice of getting up regularly, to get out of his seat and to take a walk. The other elements essential for logical consequences are all here. She did not get angry, she did not scold, there was no threat, and finally there was agreement.

Another aspect of her procedure is important. Whenever the child is inclined to do something wrong, one can suggest an intensification of his transgressions, but this in a well-regulated form. When a child wants to chew gum, one gives him more and makes him chew more. When children are shouting, one can make a contest as to who can shout the loudest

USE OF GROUP PRESSURE

In this example the teacher effectively utilized the comments of other children in the group to provide a consequence for the child:

Example 54

George, a six-year-old in first grade, would remain in his seat when the children gathered for storytime. He would try to get the children's and the teacher's attention, making noises and jumping up and down in his seat. The teacher reminded George that if he didn't wish to come with the group and wished to remain in his seat that he should remain quiet so as not to interfere with the work of the other boys and girls. But George continued to make noises and call attention to himself and would not join the group.

Finally the teacher said to the group that she felt sorry that George didn't want to join them and she felt even sorrier that George wanted to disturb everyone and would not let them do their work. She really didn't know what she could do about it and what would the children suggest? One little boy suggested that maybe George was tired and needed a rest and that was why he acted that way. The teacher asked him whether he was tired but George said he didn't know and kept on disturbing. The teacher asked the group what was the best thing to do when someone was tired, and some of the children suggested that maybe George could go to the nurse's room and go to bed and rest. The teacher took the suggestion and sent him to the nurse's office and he was put to bed. After this when George started disturbing and the children said, "Maybe George is tired again," he would stop his disturbance and start thinking about the other children around him.

The good part of the effectiveness of this technique involves the use of the group as a means of enforcing discipline. In this situation the attention George obtained from his disruption was no longer the kind he wanted because it resulted in his being excluded from the group, and also because the group did not respond in the way which he had hoped or in the way in which they had been responding before.

CLEANING UP BEFORE RECESS

The periods after the beginning of the class and before and after recess, lunchtime, and physical education are always times in which misbehavior seems more likely to happen than during the regular class period. Part of this may be due to the changes in routines, the opportunity for children to move around more than usual during the cleanup periods or afterward, or the restlessness and excitement from being outside and active, which has not yet worn off. Thorough training in routines plus alertness on the part of the teacher is necessary to keep things moving smoothly. Often, however, there are individual children who need the benefit of a consequence in order to help them to avoid the disruptions which frequently occur at this time.

Example 55

Cheryl, a fourth-grader who used charm very effectively to gain attention, also had supplementary methods—slowness, telling stories, inability to organize her desk. Whenever art or committee work preceded recess, Cheryl would still be cleaning up while the class waited in line. One day as we were standing late as usual, I had her leave her mess, go with us, and clean it up when we came back. The next day, instead of waiting until the usual time, I insisted that Cheryl begin cleaning up ten minutes ahead of the others in order to be ready on time. She protested and pleaded, but I quietly did not change my mind. She was ready early that day and the class went out on time. I regret that at that time I was very inexperienced and unaware and did not follow up on this procedure, but I am confident that it would need a logical consequence that would effectively reach Cheryl.

It would have been better to require that Cheryl not join the class group at recess until she had finished cleaning up. Unfortunately, this was impossible because many school districts have the practice of requiring teachers to act as baby-sitters on the playground and also not allowing children to be in the room unattended by teachers. The teacher's procedure seems to be a fairly effective alternative, although she could have explained her requirement by stating that since Cheryl needed more time to clean up than the other girls, it might be wise for her to start earlier.

PROBLEMS ON THE PLAYGROUND: FIGHTING

Example 56

First-grade children love to fight. At the beginning of school we have a discussion about fighting in which we come to the conclusion that they should not fight at school because the results could be serious. Here is a formula to prevent fights. If anyone fights, he is telling us he doesn't like to play with us; therefore he should leave and sit on the sidelines until he feels he can join the game without fighting. If he continues fighting, he needs more time to think it over, so it is necessary that he sit out the entire recess. The more times he fights, the longer he has to leave the game; he also realizes that no matter how quickly he comes

back, his place is lost. This almost always ends the fighting
for the year.

There is no question as to the seriousness of most playground fights among elementary school children. Generally,
school rules require that the teacher take steps to prevent
them or at least to stop them when they have started. Utilization of group discussion proves to be an effective way to
handle this for a first-grade group, as in the example just
given. Another example, a variation of the old "putting-
on-the-gloves" method, which has been tried and found
true for many years, is as follows:

Example 57

Children of Mexican-American background are quick to
fight on the playground. At home in the neighborhood they
fight as a pastime. This is not felt to be objectionable, but
at the school we are expected to prevent these battles.
Children frequently have quick tempers, and what may start
out as a friendly tussle may rapidly develop into a full-
fledged battle.

On two occasions in two different years we have had a
fight in the classroom subsequent to a fight on the playground. The offenders were asked if they wished to finish
the fight in their room. They readily agreed. It sounded like
fun. The onlookers, the rest of the class, expected a show.
They watched for a time but soon lost interest, at which
time they were given work as usual. The fighters alternately
slowed down and mixed it up. The match lasted eight to
ten minutes, at which time the spirits of the participants
were sagging and each agreed that he had had enough fighting. On one occasion one boy's pants began to slip, which
forced him to fight with one hand in order to preserve his
decency.

Subsequent to the match in the classroom, the fighting
on the playground was lessened, at least by members of the

class. When there was an occasional bout, they assured the teacher they did not need to finish it in the room. The fight was all over quickly.

COMING IN FROM RECESS

Example 58

I had been having a great deal of trouble getting one of my first-grade boys to line up with the rest of the class at the end of recess. Of several methods of correction I had tried, none seemed to have any effect on him. Finally, on one occasion he stayed on the monkey bars for some time after I had blown my whistle. All the other children obeyed the signal and took their place in line. The one child missing was at the height of his glory. This was an excellent way for him to get added attention.

I called the boy over and asked him to tell me the rules for lining up. This he did. I then asked if he had followed those rules. His answer was negative. When asked if he would rather remain outside or go with the rest of the class, he quickly chose the first. Much to his surprise, I told him this was fine with me and when he wanted to come and work with the other children, he could return to the classroom. The rest of us went in and had been working only a short time when he quietly passed through the door and took his seat. To this day he has not failed to line up on time.

Perhaps one of the most interesting aspects of this particular consequence was the comments by a group of teachers who had been asked to evaluate it as to its effectiveness. They agreed that it was a good logical consequence, but added that the teacher should never have left the child unattended on the bars; he could have been injured. This illustrates a rather distressing and growing phenomenon which characterizes the behavior of most school administrators. Motivated primarily by the fear of lawsuits from parents, school districts generally have adopted the rule that no child should be unattended anywhere at school—even in the washroom by themselves! Virtually every moment the child spends at school must be under the supervision of a teacher or a teacher's aide. As a result, the degree of regimentation is truly frightening in some instances. In most cases children are expected to march out on the playground like little military marionettes, to play only games which the teacher prescribes, and march back in.

In some instances there are rules forbidding talking with one another during lunchtime, although enforcement of such an idiotic edict has been somewhat less than successful. Perhaps an extreme example was observed by one of the authors in a California high school where a cubicle was installed with a one-way glass pane in order that the boys' washroom be kept under surveillance at all times. Whether these practices are merely a symptom of or result of the utter bankruptcy of schools in attempting to control children is difficult to ascertain. At the same time, it merely increases the contempt and defiance of children who recognize these rules as arbitrary and unreasonable demands on their privacy and their ability to function in a responsible manner. The following example is perhaps a good case in point to illustrate this:

USE OF LAVATORY

Example 59

Every morning at ten-twenty the first-grade class was escorted to the lavatory. The teacher thought this was a good procedure because it minimized the request for permission to go to the lavatory during class time. About midsemester the teacher noticed that Jim would request permission to go to the boys' room about five minutes after the class had returned from their excursion. After the third consecutive day of these requests, the teacher decided to start the art period at that time. When Jim returned to the room, the class was set up for painting. Jim asked for his painting materials so that he could paint, and the teacher told him that they were all distributed and that he would have to miss painting that day. The following day Jim did not request permission to go to the boys' room but stayed in the class and received his painting materials along with the rest of the class. About ten minutes later the teacher noticed a puddle beneath Jim's chair. It appears somewhat likely that Jim was responding to the teacher's autocratic demands on the class as an act of retaliation.

Although often repeated requests to go to the lavatory are a type of attention-getting as well as attempts to avoid certain kinds of unpleasant work, regulating the bathroom habits of the entire class would seem to be an inadequate method of solving the problem. Children are resourceful in defeating the teacher despite all regulations. It would have been far better for the teacher to have dealt with such a disturbance as a problem to be discussed by the class and resolved by common agreement.

PHYSICAL EDUCATION— NOT PLAYING THE GAME

A very common characteristic of children who misbehave is failure to play the game properly or attempt to indulge in various disturbing behaviors during the game.

Example 60

During a preschool rhythm class of four-year-olds, Danny, seeking attention consistently, insisted on being different from the rest of the group. When we played circle games, no matter what the child was supposed to be doing, Danny ignored instructions to remain in the circle. He would leave his place and start skipping around the group. Finally I asked him if he wanted to play with the group and take turns or skip around the circle. He said he wanted to skip. I immediately changed to a series of games that used a child in the center and ignored him. For a while he skipped away and tried to get attention by singing louder than the group. The other children raised their voices and drowned him out. When we sat down to do some finger plays, Danny wanted to join us. I reminded him that he had made a choice and had decided not to play with the group that day. Then I told him that if he was tired and wanted to sit down, he could go outside and sit, but he couldn't join the class anymore that day. He walked aimlessly around the room for a minute and left. Since then, the few times he has forgotten and made a similar bid for attention, I have only had to ask him if he wanted to play with the group or by himself.

It was correct to give Danny a choice, but the extension of the period was arbitrarily imposed by the teacher. Usually when the child chooses to excuse himself from the group, it is not long before he realizes its disadvantage.

Rules formulated by the group also are effective as consequences, as the following example suggests:

Example 61

Sam, a nine-year-old fourth-grader is an intelligent boy who demands more than his share of attention. When his team is at bat, he is eager for his turn to show off. However, when it is his turn to play in the field, he finds many things to do such as get a drink, go to the lavatory, go to see the nurse. His teammates became tired of Sam's dodging his part in the work and asked me to help set up a set of rules. After a period of discussion, it was agreed that anyone leaving the area when the team was in the field would also lose his next turn at bat. After trying his old tricks for several days and finding that his teammates refused to let him break the rule, Sam became willing to do his part in the field to earn his turn at bat.

STAYING AFTER SCHOOL

One of the most common "punishments" in the old-time school was requiring that the student stay after school. This punishment was invoked for a wide variety of misbehaviors and often with the additional requirement that the student laboriously write down five hundred times "I am a bad boy" or to do extra assignments which merely increased his distaste and dislike for schoolwork. The advent of the school bus has all but removed this weapon from the teacher as a means of enforcing conformity. However, as the following example will illustrate, a resourceful teacher found a way to utilize a consequence even though there was a bus trip involved.

Example 62

John, a third-grader of better than average ability, frequently played around during worktime and did not finish his assignments. Since the primary children rode a special bus which left at 3 P.M., the children who were transported by bus were rarely asked to stay after school. One day I explained to John that if he did not use the schooltime to complete his work, it would be necessary for him to do it after school. He confidently informed me that he had to ride the bus. I explained that I could make arrangements for him to ride on a later bus and call his mother so she wouldn't worry. The next time an assignment was given which he made no effort to finish, I reminded him at dismissal that I expected him to remain after school. He burst into loud sobs and begged to go home on the early bus.

I left the room to make the bus arrangements and call his mother. When I returned he was hard at work completing his assignment. As a result he began to take a great deal more responsibility in using the class work periods effectively.

Although the teacher told the child in advance what would happen if he failed to compete his work, John refused to believe her. It is clear that the teacher did not threaten or punish. She remained firm but quiet. One can be firm only if one is quiet. Otherwise a power struggle is inevitable. The teacher skillfully avoided this and remained friendly. Few teachers are able to do this without special training in this approach.

Another example from an earlier writing also shows how effectively the teacher removed the punitive aspect of such a procedure, by helping to gain the child's confidence as well as solve the problem:

Example 63

Peter fiddled during arithmetic. "You can do it now or you can do it after school," I told him. Peter didn't say much and continued to play around, waste time, and glance around the room. After the arithmetic period ended, Peter turned in his paper with only one problem on it and this did not have the right answer. I told him he must stay after school to complete his work. He didn't say anything. After school I returned Peter's paper and told him to finish his work. He said he couldn't stay; he had to go uptown. "I'm sorry, but you know your work must be done," I told him. "I have to go home," he insisted. "You can leave as soon as your work is done." Peter took the paper to his seat and after an outburst of tears, cried violently. I said, "I know how you feel. I would like to go home, too. But when the work isn't finished, I must stay until it's done." Peter continued to cry and would raise his head now and then to look up at me. After a while he stopped crying, and in a relatively short time he completed his problems and got every answer right except one.[5]

In this case the teacher's remark about understanding how he felt, identifying him with herself—she, too, would like to go home but had to finish her work first—were the crucial words in a crucial moment. They removed her from a position of authority and established order as an authority above both of them. They indicated a humbleness which did not diminish her firmness.

DEFACING SCHOOL PROPERTY

Perhaps one of the most common methods of defacing school property is doodling on the desk. Some of the more destructive children, usually boys, take great delight in carving their initials or other types of drawings on the desk top. In the following case the teacher found a rather ingenious way of solving the desk-defacing problem:

Example 64

I observed a sixth-grade student writing on his desk with pencil. His goal may have been to get my attention because I had told him numerous times in front of the class that it would have to be discontinued. I am, however, inclined to think it was just a habit which the child had developed over a period of three or four years and was finding it almost impossible to stop. I told the boy numerous times over a three-week period that it would have to be discontinued and I explained why. Most of the other students usually heard me talking to him about "desk writing."

[5] *Ibid.*, p. 86.

After about three weeks I told him that I would have to find some other means to help him correct the bad habit. The next time he wrote on the desk, I had him stay during recess and put classified newspaper advertisements upside down on his desk. We taped them to the underside of the desk so it was neat and tightly drawn. I told him that we would leave it there for a few days, and if it was neat at the end of that time, we would remove it; otherwise we would have to find some other way to protect the desk. In my opinion this was a logical consequence, because after the paper was removed, the pencil writing was no longer a problem. The boy knew why we were taping the newspapers on the desk. It appeared to me the boy greatly disliked not having the varnished surface on which to work; he also lost prestige in having a different kind of desk top. He thought the others were watching him while the papers were on the desk because he was a sloppy housekeeper, and I have not had to speak to a single student about writing for the past two months.

It is interesting to note that though this teacher was able to solve this problem once she had hit upon an effective method, she still did not know what was going on. She thought that it was "just a habit," not recognizing the power struggle in which the child had involved her. Her earlier, futile attempts to solve it followed the usual tradition of exhortation, scolding, preaching, and explaining what the boy already knew. However, telling him that his activity "would have to be discontinued" is obviously mere wishful thinking on the part of the teacher. As a result she could not understand the reason why her efforts were futile. When she substituted actions for her words she was effective, because she disinvolved herself from fighting with the boy. There was no fun in writing on the newspaper—nobody would have tried to stop the boy.

GUM CHEWING

Example 65

While observing a sixth-grade class I was told by the regular teacher about Tommy. For two mornings he brought gum to school and chewed it in class all day. Each day the teacher made him throw the gum in the wastebasket, told him the rules, and gave him the reasons for not chewing gum in the class. But as soon as the teacher returned to the class work, Tommy would again put a piece of gum in his mouth and start chewing it.

The morning I went to observe this class the teacher related the story to me and said she was going to try something she should have done the very first day.

When Tommy came into the room, he had his gum in his mouth. The teacher asked him if he wanted to be alone and chew gum, or be with the class and not chew gum. Tommy answered that he wanted to chew his gum. He was then told to take his chair to a single table at the back of the class, and was given three pieces of double bubble gum. The teacher's instructions were: He must sit at the table alone until recess and chew all three pieces of bubble gum at one time.

After about thirty minutes or so Tommy asked whether he could throw away the gum because his jaws were tired. The teacher said he could not until recess time. After recess Tommy was again given the same choice as before. This time he stayed with the class without gum.

At lunchtime the teacher showed me a bagful of bubble gum and explained that she was prepared to give Tommy four pieces of gum and make him chew them till lunchtime had he again preferred chewing gum.

Was this an application of logical consequences? It almost was. The teacher was on the right track, but spoiled the effect, by turning a possible logical consequence into arbitrary punishment. The fact that the results were good does not make it a correct procedure. There are two questions involved in this story: Why was it not logical consequence, and why did it work?

As soon as the teacher gave the order to "make" the boy chew a number of pieces at the same time and forced him to do that for a specific length of time, she violated one principle of correct application. She could have succeeded had she merely given the boy a choice to chew his gum for himself at the back of the class, or stop chewing it and join the class, which the boy was ready to do after half an hour. He asked whether he could throw away the gum. And this was the decision for which the teacher should have been striving. This example shows a clear-cut dictatorial and arbitrary procedure which is, both in technique and in spirit, alien to the procedure of logical consequences.

Why, then, was her approach effective? Because she stopped telling the rules, giving the reasons, explaining and talking, which she had done before, and suddenly moved into action. Children always respond to action better than to words. And this is the reason why he gave up chewing the gum, at least on this occasion. It is rather doubtful that this procedure made the boy more willing to observe rules.

There is, of course, another element which worked in favor of the teacher. She turned the pleasant sensation of chewing gum into a most unpleasant chore and assignment. The value of such an approach should not be underestimated. If the teacher is creative enough to bring about an utterly unexpected situation, she has a chance to impress the child. Still, this does not make the example one of logical consequences properly applied.

The following indicates how a similar situation was handled without the need for arbitrary conditions:

Example 66

During the fourth week of school this semester Joe started coming to class with gum in his mouth. He didn't chew just one stick at a time but four or five. I mentioned to him that gum wasn't allowed in class but I did not tell him to remove his gum because it was evident that he was using it as an attention-getting device. Gum chewing continued and Joe was given the choice of chewing gum all the time or being like the rest of the students. He chose to chew gum constantly. By the end of the class period he was rather tired of chewing. Nothing was said about gum chewing for the following week and Joe did not chew gum in class anymore.

This is another example of the technique described earlier of allowing the child to continue his behavior until thoroughly tired of it. In this case it was agreed from the start that once he chose chewing he would have to continue it for the whole day. There is no fun in doing what is not forbidden. This technique is useful in a wide variety of situations such as the example of spitting which follows:

Example 67

Two boys spit at each other during recess. After recess they were asked to spit but not at each other. The class sat on the grass while the two boys spat, got dry, and spat again. This took seven or eight minutes until their "spitters" were really tired. This ended the spitting on one another at school.

A somewhat similar method was used by a teacher in dealing with rock throwing on the playground.

Example 68

When I was on yard duty, several boys were throwing rocks at the far end of the playground. I blew my whistle and had them come to me. Then I noticed that they did this without much complaint and were very meek as they approached. I felt that their behavior was based on a power struggle, not with me, but with the rules in general. They were probably just seeing how far they could go. I told them I knew they knew the rules so I didn't have to repeat them. They agreed with this, so I asked them if they could see any reason why they shouldn't throw rocks on the playground. Naturally, they came up with all the right answers. I said this proved to me that they really decided the pleasure they got from throwing the rocks was worth the consequences that might come from breaking the rules. This brought smiles to their faces. I continued; rather than discourage them from throwing rocks, I suggested they use this rock throwing in a constructive way that would help the whole school. Now interested, they listened as I pointed out all the rocks that filled the playground. I said they should gather as many as they could, walk to the fence and throw them up over the fence into a neighboring field so as not to hit anyone accidentally by bouncing stones off the fence or something like that. They were then told to report to me how many they had thrown after recess. I also told them any time they felt like throwing rocks during recess, I would be more than happy to let them do that. I have not seen a rock thrown by any one of the boys or any of the other children since.

There are several important implications revealed in this teacher's report. From the beginning she effectively revealed to the children their goal of power, that is, to get away with breaking of the school rules. The evidence has indicated that when the correct goal of misbehavior is revealed, children often reconsider their behavior. The teacher, even when tested further, avoided the trap of forbidding them to throw rocks, but gave them the opportunity to divert this pastime into a constructive channel. Although the report does not state whether the boys actually spent any time throwing rocks over the wall as she had suggested, this apparently effectively ended the rock throwing as far as she could ascertain.

BITING

Though not a common misbehavior, children do bite one another in the primary grades. The following was reported by a school vice-principal:

Example 69

Joan, a kindergarten student in a private school, was the oldest of two children in a very wealthy servant-run family. All year the teacher had had trouble with her biting other children. One day, after three more children had been bitten, the teacher finally sent her to me. I asked Joan why she bit other children. Was she mad at them? She said she just felt like it. She really liked the other children and wanted to play with them. We talked quietly for about five minutes and I explained that dogs, cats, and animals bit but that people didn't. After all this, Joan said that she would bite if she felt like it. I explained that when animals bit, their owners were required to put up a sign telling others of the danger and I thought that since she still felt she would bite other children we must do the same thing to her. I made a small sign that read "I Bite People" and pinned it to her dress and told her that when she felt she could keep from biting, we would take the sign off. Joan wore the sign all day and even wore it home. The next day Joan's parents came storming to school. They said that I had caused a great psychological trauma in their child— in fact, all hell broke loose. I still don't know how else I could have handled the situaton. There were no more biting episodes the rest of the year.

This shows ingenuity on the part of the vice-principal and also courage to face what one might call a typical parent reaction. It seems likely that the parents had not really faced the issue of the child's determination to have her own way and to believe that she has the right to do whatever she liked. The parents apparently under some psychological influence objected to the teacher not respecting this right of their child. It takes more than the average amount of forbearance and courage to handle and resist parental pressures when the teacher tries to offset the influence of the home.

CHAPTER 7

Logical Consequences With Adolescents

A. IN THE FAMILY

Much has been written and spoken about the greatly increased difficulties and perplexities in dealing with adolescents as compared to younger children. There are, of course, many valid reasons for this. Numerous parents and teachers fail to see that the reactions and attitudes of adolescents are much closer to those of adults than to children. Indeed, in earlier cultures and in some primitive societies today, children were considered ready to accept adult responsibility at the time of puberty. In their zeal to "protect" children, today's adults have created what might be called a twilight zone, wherein the adolescent is really neither a child nor an adult but a confused and often frustrated mixture of both. However, as the examples given will show, both at home and in the classroom, logical consequences are generally far more effective in dealing with adolescents than are the conventional type of punishments which adults still feel constrained to inflict upon them. Though their basic attitudes are not as easily altered as are those of younger children, all but the most severely disturbed can learn from the natural consequences of their own acts, if they are properly confronted with them. Consequences with adolescents are more difficult because of the power struggle which is nearly always present between adolescents and adults in today's society. The war between the generations reaches its peak during this period.

CHORES AROUND THE HOUSE

Enforcing rules regarding the completion of assigned chores around the home is as difficult with adolescents as with children, or perhaps even more so. Utilization of the family council and the natural consequences which can grow out of it thus are indispensable, as the following example shows:

Example 70

A pattern seemed to be established on mother's part that she was spending most of Saturday nagging the children to do the tasks that had been established for each of them in the family council. Realizing what she was doing, she brought up this matter at the family council saying that the nagging was wearing her down and creating much friction in the family group. She asked if the family could jointly find a solution to the problem. After much discussion it was decided that the responsibility should not be even mentioned by mother but that all tasks must be finished by four o'clock every Saturday. In other words, the children had the freedom to choose when on Saturday, morning or afternoon, they would take care of their tasks.

The following Saturday three of the children went merrily about doing their jobs. Jim, the fourth one, decided to play basketball with his buddy. Then he watched a TV program until lunch. Incidentally, he had been the one whom mother had to nag the most. This time she said nothing. At 2 P.M. mother and father decided to take the children to the beach for a few hours. Much to Jim's dismay, he was unable to join them because he still had the lawn to mow. He asked if he could wait and mow the lawn on Monday after school; but the decision of the family council held. He stayed home and mowed the lawn while the family went to the beach. The following Saturday, Jim made sure he completed his task before he played basketball and watched TV.

Although this decision had not been discussed at the family council, the logic of the parents' action was sufficiently plain so that Jim did not repeat his misbehavior, and his chores were done before he wanted to play or watch TV.

Example 71

My two teen-age daughters chose to leave the dishes for their mother. I left them until time for another meal. I prepared the meal in an untidy kitchen and announced the meal was ready. The girls found enough clean dishes to set the table. After the meal they took off and left the house and dishes in a mess. I left the house also and did not return until after suppertime. Everybody was home in a dirty mess with no meal and no mother. The girls reaped the consequence by washing the mess of dry, smelling dishes before a meal was prepared. They now say, "The sooner the dishes are washed, the better." This lesson is several years old, but remains fresh in ther minds.

This example illustrates a rather important point which is essential in all relationships with children, particularly with teen-agers. Although you cannot force them to do what they choose not to do, neither can they force you to do anything. As the children did not carry out their part of the bargain of washing the dishes, mother indicated by her absence that she would not prepare the meal until there were clean dishes on which to serve it. In nearly all such instances, even adolescents can be made to realize that cooperation is a two-way street. There are many services that they expect and demand; these could be withheld when they do not cooperate, but not on a this-for-that basis, as retaliation, but as a logical and understandable consequence, as the following example illustrates:

Example 72

Through use of the family council, a system of dividing up chores was arranged. In most instances both Sally, age fifteen, and Gloria, age thirteen, seemed to fulfill their assignments reasonably well, except in clearing the table and dishwashing, which they both disliked. As this usually occurred just as their favorite TV programs were on, they hit on the scheme of doing their chores during the commercials and station breaks. This sometimes found them still unfinished by bedtime, and more than once mother had to remind them to complete the task before going to bed.

After thinking it over, and discussing it with her husband who was agreeable to the experiment, mother decided to take a leaf from her daughters' book and cook dinner during the commercials. She took the evening when her favorite programs were on and, as it happened, there were three in sequence. Though the children complained about being hungry, she did not answer them, except to say that she was doing it as fast as she could under the circumstances. At ten thirty the dinner was finally ready. After that there were very few lapses on completing the dishes as soon as subsequent dinners were finished.

CLEANING UP ROOMS

Next to doing chores around the house, unwillingness to tidy their rooms seems to be one of the most frequent examples of adolescent misbehavior. The following is perhaps one of the truly effective ways that has been discovered to solve the bedmaking problem.

Example 73

Jan and her older sister, Sally, share the same bedroom. Both girls have been encouraged to make their own beds and keep their room tidy and neat. Sally has done quite well and is even willing to pick up the entire room. But she refused to make Jan's bed when Jan wasn't interested in doing her share. Lately this led to almost daily quarreling. I believe this to be a power contest with us as well as a display of sibling rivalry. Feeling inadequate in competition with her sister, Jan resorts to negative behavior. My wife pointed this out to me, looking for an opportunity to use a logical consequence.

As Sally had on occasion gone to school with her bed unmade, I decided to give the choice to both girls. I discussed with them the necessity of having to share the same room and the responsibility of each in sharing their duties. Since the bedmaking seemed to be the central source of conflict, the discussion was soon centered on this point. I suggested that since we had that bedmaking problem, perhaps we should do something about it. I asked the girls whether they would rather have them unmade during the day or would they rather make them. Both girls decided to have their beds unmade. After they had left for school, their mother and I folded the spreads, blankets, and sheets and stacked them at the foot of their beds. Mother explained that they had chosen to have their beds unmade, it was their room to keep as they saw fit. Both promptly made their beds.

The following morning both beds were made before they left for school. The next morning Sally made hers, Jan did not. My wife removed Jan's covers to the floor. When Jan returned from school she was again upset by the developments. She promptly made her bed and has made it each morning for the past week before going to school. Even though the room has not been what you could call "ship-shape," we have made a point to praise the girls for their interest.

This would appear to be a variation of the military technique used in boot camps: When the drill sergeant sees a corner of a bed misplaced, he promptly strips the entire bed down and forces the recruit to make it completely over again. The difference is that the girls had a choice of either having their beds made or not, but did this give the mother the right to make a worse disorder? The best part of this procedure was the quiet action of the mother.

Example 74

We were having difficulty getting our thirteen-year-old daughter to hang up her clothes. She not only dropped them where she pulled them off, she seemed to delight in wadding them up. She had been pretty good about her clothes when she was younger, and we did not understand her change. After trying reasoning, threatening, and scolding, I finally told her to go ahead and throw them down; I would not pick them up for her. Furthermore, I would not iron them anymore as long as she did throw them around. So she complained she did not have enough to wear. We refused to get her more until she took care of what she had. She wore soiled and wrinkled clothes to school quite a few times before she began to be more careful. It was not long before the clothes were picked up.

Often procedures such as this are useful in getting teenagers to take over responsibilities for their clothes and their room that they had previously not been willing to assume.

WEARING PROPER CLOTHES

Example 75

My daughter Joan has a minor foot problem. The doctor prescribed oxfords with a slight built-in lift. Flats and heels were forbidden except for rare dress occasions. The physician stated that it would take four to five years to correct, an eternity in the mind of a fourteen-year-old. The whole problem was further complicated by the fact that oxfords are not exactly the height of fashion among Joan's peers. After wearing the corrective shoes a few times, Joan began to register her displeasure. One warm day she came home from school barefoot, and when I asked her why she was not wearing her shoes, she replied it was just too hot. I suspected the real reason but made no further comment. The next day when she returned from school, she was wearing her gym shoes. When I asked her why, she said she hurried from the room and had not had time to change. I called her back, and as she stared at me in injured innocence, I pointed out the inconsistency of her statement. Lacking further defense, her eyes filled with tears and she crumpled into a chair and said she just couldn't face the other girls at school wearing those "old, stupid, and ugly shoes." I told her that I could see no way in which she would not have to wear the shoes. I tried to explain the importance of the shoes to her, but it was obvious that I was making little, if any, impression on her.

After this she wore them with a great deal more regularity, but she did everything possible to let me know that she was unhappy. For instance, when she walked, she would drag her feet or scuff her heels in rather obvious effort to wear the shoes out as soon as possible. Needless to say, the shoes wou d not last long with this sort of treatment.

I finally decided that another approach to the problem would have to be taken. In analyzing the situation, I decided the reason for her noncooperation was possibly because she had not really been consulted in this whole matter. She had merely been apprised of her foot condition and taken to a doctor and told what she had to do. She had no solution to the problem; she was told to do something in a situation which she did not like, and furthermore, no one had made an effort to see what she thought about it.

Because of the duration of the treatment, I knew force

would not work and her cooperation would therefore have to be enlisted. I also knew that in most matters Joan was a rather responsible girl. So I decided to rely on past training to resolve the problem. One evening she said with a rather triumphant gleam in her eye that her oxfords were worn out and that she would need new shoes. I said that I had some shopping also and we would go together the next evening.

The following night when we arrived at the store, I gave her some money and told her to go to the shoe department and buy the shoes she would need, and that we would meet at the book counter in thirty minutes. Joan gave me a rather dubious look and asked if she had to get the same type of oxford. I said no, she could get anything that would be good for school. When Joan asked the reason for the change, I said that there was no change in her need for the oxford but we were tired of the constant argument about shoes. Later Joan arrived at the book counter and asked if it was all right if she bought a pair of white oxfords and then dyed them a bright color. When I agreed to this plan, Joan asked if I would come to the department and help her. A week later Joan was willingly dressed in what seemed to be a rather nauseating pair of oxfords, but when she came home from school the first day of wearing them, she had a rather pleased look on her face. It seemed that several of the girls not only admired the novel color of her shoes, but it was fantastic that a parent would allow anyone to do that to a brand-new pair of shoes.

When Joan discovered suddenly that the burden of responsibility to correct her foot problem rested solely on her shoulders and that no one was going to force her to wear shoes she did not like, she saw the situation in a new perspective. She was fully aware of what it would do to her feet if she did not wear corrective shoes. The nature of the whole problem appeared to have changed from how to get out of wearing them to how to make them as attractive as possible. This case illustrates some very important principles which, though applicable in all relations with children, are particularly essential in dealing with teen-agers. An almost universal complaint among parents is that teen-agers show so little responsibility regarding tasks which parents want them to do. The parents' mistake, of course, is trying to pressure them into complying. As long as Joan's parents demanded that she wear the oxfords, she was determined to defeat them in whatever way possible, although she did not openly rebel by refusing to wear them. However, as soon as the pressure was taken off and she was permitted to make her own decision regarding the problem, she was willing to make a choice dictated by common sense rather than by the desire to rebel. Although this would not be called a logical consequence in the usual sense, it indicates how important it is to leave the responsibility as much as possible for their own actions up to the children.

PUNCTUALITY

Next to doing work around the house, being places on time seems to be one of the most universal problems, but one which lends itself easily to the application of logical consequences.

Example 76

Fifteen-year-old George and twelve-year-old Joan are in a turmoil every morning preparing to leave for school by 7:30 A.M. This requires leaving ample time for showering, dressing, making beds, and eating breakfast. The latter two receive least attention. Each child has his own alarm clock and is responsible for his own awakening. Mother prepares breakfast, but she found that insufficient time was allowed by the children for eating. Frequently breakfast was either partially eaten or not at all. Recognizing the burden of getting the children to breakfast was falling on mother, this became a power struggle. Mother informed the youngsters that she would henceforth sleep later and would not prepare breakfast for them since they were obviously not interested. However, if they felt they wanted her to resume making breakfast, they must allow time to consume it. After a couple of days without mother, they requested her return and did allow more time to fulfill their duties as well as to eat breakfast and reach school on time.

As was mentioned before, cooperation is a two-way street.

Example 77

Jack, twelve years old, is frequently late for supper. Partially this is a bid for attention. However, many times he has displayed defiance by being argumentative. A week ago he arrived home an hour late for supper. An explanation was requested and he responded that his baseball team had played later than usual and that a meeting of the players was called. I explained to him that this could have been a legitimate excuse and had he phoned me or sent word home of the situation, we would not have been concerned for his safety. The ball game was played less than a block from home, so sending word would not have been difficult. Knowing how desperately hungry active growing boys are, I chose not to deny him food; I told him that he could have what was left of supper. However, other members of the family were settled down to studies and other duties, hence it would be necessary for him to take care of the kitchen chores. I might explain here that usually supper dishes are done by two or three children—one clears the table and one rinses and stacks, depending upon whose turn it is. However, because Jack was late this had been put off. Knowing his dislike of washing dishes, I fully expected a tirade from him. Without a word he ate and did an excellent job of cleaning up the kitchen. He has not been late since, without permission.

In this instance Jack could see that his tardiness would have delayed the others in their evening work, had they come back to help in the kitchen at such a late hour. Although the mother did rationalize regarding the boy's alleged inability to go without a meal, she managed to come up with an effective alternative consequence.

Example 78

Sherry, an intelligent twelve-year-old, lives a distance from junior high school. After she forgot her lunch twice the first week of school and called home for me to bring it, I decided we'd have a talk. I explained to Sherry that as we grow up we must be responsible for certain tasks and one of hers was to remember to take her lunch. She could not depend on me to bring her lunch, for sometimes I wouldn't be home and sometimes it would be inconvenient. She seemed to be listening, but the next morning after she left for school I noticed that she forgot her lunch. As I had to go shopping, it was a temptation to take her lunch on the way, but I didn't. At three thirty when she arrived home from school she was famished and wondered where I was when she called. I told her that I had to leave the house. She decided to always place her lunch next to her books so she wouldn't forget again.

Routines, such as these, are so much more easily enforced when unaccompanied by the usual scoldings about the forgetfulness. It is to be emphasized that all of this could have been accomplished without the incessant reminders and explanations.

USE OF AUTOMOBILES

Perhaps one of the most perplexing problems with which parents are faced is how to deal with the adolescent's desire to use and own a car. The pressure is very great on the parent because the adolescent regards owning or driving a car both as a status symbol of being grown up and as an increase in his freedom and mobility. But he often does not handle the car properly, and in addition to bearing the burden of increased insurance cost, the parent is also liable for any transgression that the teen-ager might commit. As can be seen in this crucial area, logical consequences may work in some instances, not as well in others.

Example 79

A boy aged seventeen has a steady job and earns about $40 a week. He wanted to buy a car and finance it through a loan company. It was a 1955 Chevrolet with many extras, popular with teen-agers at this time. The car would cost $695, the insurance $265 a year. The boy talked it over with his parents who suggested that he look before leaping into such an expensive venture, but to decide for himself since he would be making the payments. The boy had the car two days and found out that he had to pay $446 for repairs, checked further and found many other things wrong with it. He took the car back to the dealer from whom he purchased it and received only $500 for it. This left him a balance of $195 plus high interest which he had to pay to the loan company until his debt was cleared.

In this case the parents stayed out of it and allowed the boy to handle the situation entirely by himself. It is obvious that the next time he tries to get a car he will be more careful.

Example 80

> John often drives the family car at excessive speed. One
> morning at 5:30 A.M. he rolled the family station wagon
> over three times on the road to a popular mountain resort.
> He and his two passengers were unhurt except for a few
> scratches; the car was a total loss. His father, arriving two
> hours later, remained relatively calm. No punishment was
> administered at the time; he was shown how the accident
> was directly attributable to the high speed at which he was
> driving. The parent explained to him how his speed could
> have caused serious monetary reprisals from his passengers
> in the form of injury suits. They were unhurt, but their
> parents would not sign injury releases. He paid off the
> deductible portion of the insurance—$100—and had to
> pay increased insurance premiums. His use of the other
> family car was curtailed until such time as the father
> thought he had proper respect for the rules of driving.

There seems considerable question as to whether all
these elaborate attempts to "explain" the consequences of
his act were of any real value after the accident had occurred. Perhaps it would have been wise to have explained
all this before he started to use the family car. The boy
still drives too fast. This is probably due to two factors.
First, at the time of the accident he was accompanied by
two friends for whom he tends to show off. He was, by his
own admission, trying to show them how the car would
"run." The wreck did not appear to have the desired effect.
The accident was not enough to slow the boy down.

Perhaps the parent could have said that if he had any
evidence that the boy had been still driving at excessive
speeds, the car would be taken away for a longer period of
time, then given back to him with the understanding that if
he was ready to drive the car at reasonable speed he could
then continue to use it. If not, he would not have the use

of the car. Eventually, it would seem that if this did not
have an effect, the boy would be unable to drive the family
car at all. In view of the risk involved, there would seem
to be no alternative to the father unless the boy were willing
to change his driving habits. Though in most situations
adolescents need to learn the consequences of their own act
by experience, perhaps because of the danger to others involved in the improper use of a car this may be an exception. If the adolescent cannot use an automobile properly,
he simply should not be allowed to drive it, regardless of his
resentment.

DECISION-MAKING

Decision-making should be a mutual task. In situations
involving danger to other people, such as driving an automobile at excessive or dangerous speeds, parents are responsible for the consequences. However, they should let the
youngster participate in finding the proper solutions. The
following is an interesting example of how a parent utilized
this successfully:

Example 81

My sister's child, a boy seventeen years old, did not want
to go to school in the fall and finish the last year in high
school. He wanted to join the Navy. His mother could not
understand this sudden rebellion because he had been fairly
easy to control during most of the years growing up. He was
"a model child," she would tell her friends. Lately, however, she had been telling them how different he had become
—sort of a nuisance and a show-off. She even had some
complaints from his teachers about this. The child's father
died when he was twelve. This may have had some bearing
on the situation since the mother had then to do all the
disciplining of the children and felt sorry for them, trying
to make up for the loss. She was very upset about this

behavior, afraid that he would run away from home and do something terrible and get in trouble with the police. I told her perhaps she should let him choose either to finish school or join the Navy. At least, if he decided to go in the Navy she would know where he was and he would be taken care of. She thought this over for a few days; and when he mentioned the Navy to her again, she said, "Okay, you get your good suit out, get ready and we'll go down to the recruiting office and I'll sign you into the Navy." He was a bit surprised, but he got ready anyway. All the way down she tried to explain that he wouldn't be able to do as he pleased in the Navy, but he paid little attention to her. When they walked into the recruiting office she said to the officer, "I brought this boy down to sign him into the Navy. I'm sick and tired of listening to him say he wants to go in the Navy every time I want him to do something he doesn't want to, particularly to finish high school."

Apparently the officer understood what she meant, because while he was filling in the application he was telling the boy some things he would not be able to do, such as shore leave—he wouldn't be able to go ashore until all the higher officers went ashore, and he might be in the Navy three years before he got a chance to go ashore. When the boy asked if he could finish high school in the Navy, the officer told him that he could not for three years. His mother told me that the officer really let the boy "have it" whenever he had a chance during the filling out of the application.

When it was all completed, the officer asked Jack to sign it. Jack said that he would like to think about it for awhile. "Okay," said the officer, "I'll be back in a few minutes." When the officer had gone, Jack looked at his mother and said, "What should I do, Mother?" She told him it was his decision and that he could do what he liked. When the officer came back, he pushed the paper at Jack and said, "Okay, son, you sign here and then your mother can sign just below your signature."

Jack looked at the paper a minute and then said, "I've changed my mind. I don't want to sign it."

The officer said, "You mean you have taken up my time filling out this application and you won't sign it?" Jack said he was sorry but he guessed he would finish high school first.

The officer said, "Okay, you come back in a year when you've finished high school and we'll be glad to sign you up in the Navy."

My sister told me that he was very thoughtful and quiet all the way home. He ate his lunch and went on to school.

This happened about a month ago and she hasn't heard "Join the Navy" since and he has been like a different boy, more like himself. His mother told me his schoolwork has improved as well and is almost as good as before this all happened. She also said she has said nothing more about the situation since they left the recruiting office that day.

Although the boy did not experience a consequence but only its possibility, faced with the reality of the situation and not able to use it as a means of rebelling against his mother, he quickly made a more commonsense decision.

As has been indicated, utilization of logical consequences with adolescents is far more complex and difficult than with younger children. At the same time, when the decision is left to them, their attitudes are often far more sensible than most adults would believe. Often a logical consequence is the only way to convince an adolescent that a particular behavior is not best for him. Because of his rebellion against adult authority, anything the parent suggests will usually be opposed, regardless of what it is. Consequently, the main task of the parent is to present the alternatives in such a way that the adolescent feels that he is not merely giving in to the adult demands but making his own decision.

B. IN THE SCHOOL

Dealing with adolescents in the school setting is very different from at home; yet the behavioral dynamics can be quite similar. The most common misbehaviors of secondary school students by and large involve unwillingness to do required work, showing off and other destructive behavior in class, or minor infractions such as lateness, failure to bring proper equipment, failure to utilize tools and materials in the proper manners. Though logical consequences are more difficult to administer to teen-agers, their effectiveness is heightened by the fact that other types of conventional punishment or autocratic imposition invoke far more defiance and destructiveness from adolescents than from younger children. A consequence is often more effective because it avoids the power struggle between the teacher and the student in which both sides usually lose.

THE SHOW-OFF

Example 82

One of the boys in my math class has been an annoyance all year. He disturbs the classroom by making unwanted noises, such as tapping his foot or pencil. He stops after a stern look or frown from me. Occasionally I have to tell him to quit. It seems to be an unconscious action on his part. He's apologetic each time. His classwork is better than average. Recently, my patience limited, I told him with a raised voice never to tap his pencil again. The next day after finishing a test early, he began flapping the cover of his book. I ignored this act for the longest time, hoping he would stop of his own accord. He never let up. I finally told him, and told him calmly, that he earned a five in citizenship, and he appeared hurt and angry.

This is a typical example of the usual response of a teacher to a boy who is creating a disturbance in the class. She did not understand his "unconscious" goal, here first demanding attention, and then allowed herself to become involved in a power struggle. Though the stern reprimands succeeded in stopping the pencil-tapping, it was not very long before the boy evolved a new way to annoy the teacher and distract the class. In a similar situation, another teacher handled the problem as follows:

Example 83

A seventh-grader was in the habit of tapping with his pencil on the desk whenever the teacher was attempting to conduct a social studies class. After trying numerous remedies unsuccessfully, the teacher finally hit upon the idea of giving the child a black crayon to use instead of a pencil, stating, that if he could not use the pencil correctly he would have to write with this, as the tapping of it would not make as much noise and the class would not be disrupted. The next day he asked for his pencil back and there were no more tappings.

Though perhaps this particular technique would not work with older students, it was at least effective in the case illustrated. Again the teacher tries to solve the problem by herself instead of bringing it up for class discussion. After all, it is not only the teacher who is disturbed by the boy's actions.

Example 84

John, a student in my tenth-grade class, had numerous irritating ways of showing off—making funny faces, acting the clown, and not participating in a class activity. I finally decided to try a new tactic. In calling him up after the class period, I informed him in a friendly voice that he was free to leave the class because he did not consider himself part of the group. When he felt he could return to the class and behave as the other students, he would be welcome to return. The next morning he appeared at class and asked me what he was supposed to do. I told him it was up to him and he left. After school he returned and told me that he wanted to stay in the class and that he wished to take part in the activities. After that there was very little more trouble from him.

In this case the teacher took a risk. Students who see no value in schoolwork would welcome the opportunity to loiter in the halls or in one way or another to avoid the proper class activity. Because of this, most secondary schools have rules against loitering. In this case the teacher sensed the boy would evidently become upset if he missed too much and the consequence was effective for that reason. And it was a real "consequence" and not punishment because the boy had to decide for himself whether to participate or be absent.

The following example was more soundly worked out and would consequently involve much less risk, if any at all, on the part of the teacher.

Example 85

Joe was a time-waster and a general nuisance in typing class. He was warned by the teacher that he would either have to make better use of his time and quit bothering the others or he would have to leave the class. After several warnings he was told to go to the office and to remain until the teacher came. With the support of the principal, the teacher gave the student the choice of either coming back to class and behaving as the other students or going to the study hall until he was ready to come back and conform. After two weeks in the study hall the student approached the teacher and asked if he could return to the class. This also meant the student had two weeks of work to make up, either at noon or after school hours. For the rest of the year the teacher did not have any problem with this student.

Use of group pressure from other children can also often be effective in quelling the nuisance, as in the following:

Example 86

One of my typing students, Sam, was making a bid for attention. He would tear his paper out of the machine and make a big show when he made an error. Everybody would look at him and sympathize. I ignored him. Soon this pattern was carried out to the timed writing we had twice a week. The students were given two timed writings on Tuesday and Thursday and were asked to hand in the best of the four. Sam would type for a minute or two and then rip the timed writing out of the machine and mutter comments. This would disturb the students near him, causing them to make errors, lose their place, or else hamper their progress. Neither he nor they would have an acceptable paper to hand in after such incidents. Since he was doing something wrong, I decided to utilize the group to help him rather than tell him not to do these things.

The students around him became very unhappy with his actions and were beginning to let him know it. I decided to bring the situation to a head by increasing the number of times we would have timed writings. I announced to the class that this week we were going to work on speed and would have two timed writings each day, and I would take a grade per day instead of one per week. The first day Sam again ripped the paper out of his machine and did it again the second day. The beginning of the third day I observed several of his neighbors talking to him, and I knew we were on our way. The first timed writing went off without incident, but on the second he again ripped his paper out. That did it. The students around him raised their arms and demanded loud and clear that he discontinue his distractions. I took this opportunity to conduct a class discussion on the rights and privileges of class members. He feigned surprise at anyone being disturbed. The class felt that if he could not follow the rules of the class, he should not be allowed to participate. I asked him if he felt the choice between staying in class and completing the timed writing or sitting outside the classroom while the others completed the timed writing was a fair choice. He and the class agreed that it was.

The next day I started preparations for a timed writing. Sam put a clean piece of typing paper in his machine, turned to the correct page, and waited for the signal to start. I said nothing to him about a choice, but I felt that he had indicated which one he had made. He completed both timed writings that day and did not cause any difficulty the rest of the year. As a matter of fact, it seemed to be a good learning experience for the entire class, for it became my most cooperative class. I found that after this experience Sam was a more cooperative member of all his classes.

The teacher, as could be expected, was unable to get Sam to cease his destructive behavior on his own; therefore he called upon the other members of the class to aid him by their disapproval of the action. As it turned out, this was all that was needed to get him to change his behavior. With adolescents, peer attitudes are crucial and usually far more effective than any disciplinary procedures which the teacher might attempt.

FAILING TO COMPLETE ASSIGNMENTS

Next to showing off, this is probably the most common school problem—perhaps even more so with adolescents than with younger children. In a wide variety of ways many students try to avoid doing their work. In the ensuing example, skipping school was used as the excuse:

Example 87

Last year I had a student who often skipped school. One Friday he missed the oral reading of a one-act play. I told him that I knew he skipped and otherwise ignored him. Later during a test he came up and said, "I wasn't here when we read this." I replied, "I'm sorry, John, but you had your choice of coming to school or not and getting the assignment or not. Maybe the next time you'll think before you skip the class."

In this case the teacher spoiled the consequence by preaching. Often the "I-told-you-so" attitude merely intensifies the determination of the student to defeat the teacher the next time again. A more effective approach is illustrated in the following example:

Example 88

A seventh-grade girl was particularly fond of art; she began to do her artwork not only during art period, but also in other class periods. One day while the class was working on an assignment, I noticed that she was drawing. I asked her if she would rather draw than do the assignment. She answered she would. I then went to a supply cabinet, got a package of drawing paper, and asked her to come to the table in the corner of the room. I told her she could sit at this table and draw until she felt like doing what the rest of the class was doing. For about fifteen minutes she sat at the table and did very little drawing. She then raised her hand and asked if she could return to her seat. I asked her if she was ready to do the assigned work; she was. After class she apologized for not following the directions and said it would not happen again.

In this case there was a minimum of talk and disruption of the routine of the class. As soon as the girl realized that her failure to complete the assignment was not producing the desired result, she quickly decided to rejoin the class. However, one has to be careful with children who have little or no interest in the assigned classwork. In such cases, allowing them to do what they want may be only an invitation to avoid doing what they are supposed to do. The main clue would appear to be how interested the student is in grades or how much he wants to be part of the group. In such cases this kind of consequence is quite effective.

In the next example the teacher was perhaps a little daring, but achieved a highly effective result.

Example 89

Jim, a fifteen-year-old, is in the tenth grade. He lives with his mother who separated from his father while Jim was quite young. Jim's mother works and he is left more or less on his own with no supervision at home. At school Jim is a persistent troublemaker. Although he is a good leader, he more often than not leads in the wrong direction. He is a central figure in a group clique of eight or ten boys. For several days now Jim has been bringing comic books and reading these books in class. When the teacher asks Jim to put away the comic books and pay attention to him, he will answer, "Okay, teacher, as soon as I finish this page," and continue to read. In the past the teacher has not made an issue since Jim will after a few minutes put away the comic book. This does not disrupt the class, but does not solve Jim's problem.

One day the teacher asked if Jim would rather read comic books than the text. Jim, of course, answered Yes. Then the teacher asked if Jim would like to share his comics with the class by reading them to everyone. Jim again answered Yes. After he finished reading the first story, he was ready to stop and sit down; however, the teacher had him finish reading the entire book. The teacher then produced several other comic books and had Jim read these to the class also. Forty-five minutes and several comic books later, Jim was apparently ready to swear off comic books. He has not been a major problem since.

There will be some who will complain that this was an unnecessary waste of time for the whole class. Those who do are losing sight of one essential principle. The teacher had already spent a good deal of time and a certain amount of class disruption in unsuccessful attempts to get Jim to cease his comic book reading. Since this method evidently stopped Jim's attention-getting behavior for the rest of the semester, it would indicate that the time was well spent. Often such a departure from the usual routine has a salutary effect on other potential troublemakers as well. Once the teacher demonstrates his ability to cope effectively with the problems of one child, other potential disturbers may be more careful to avoid similar provocations.

FAILURE TO PAY ATTENTION

It is sometime difficult to detect whether students who fail to heed instructions or to carry out assignments are doing this to get attention or want to show their power to do anything they want without anyone stopping them. In either case certain consequences can be effective.

Example 90

> When the teacher in a woodshop class announced he was checking out plane irons to the class, one boy would never pay attention until the tool locker was closed and the teacher had to open it up again. One day when the boy did this, the teacher was busy and did not have time to unlock the door, keeping busy the whole period. One episode like this was enough. Next day the boy was on time to get his tools.

Consequences of this sort are relatively easy to apply, but again have to be carefully planned.

Example 91

> In my seventh- and eight-grade food preparation classes I established the rule that a girl must have her apron in order to cook. When a girl does not have her apron she is relegated to such tasks as setting the table, where she does not have to work in the kitchen. This use of logical consequences works in two ways. First, the girl is disappointed that she is not allowed to be a cook. Secondly, her cooking group is inconvenienced and put behind schedule since jobs have to be reassigned.

Though this apparently was successful, the rules were laid out in an arbitrary way; this was punishment, not a consequence. Here is what might seem to be a more effective way of handling a similar situation:

Example 92

> About a week before we were beginning our cooking unit in the home economics class, I asked the girls what a cook would need in the way of equipment to protect her clothing and so on. We agreed that everyone would bring an apron, hot-dish pad, and a hand towel. On the appointed day all

but two arrived with the needed equipment. Since they had not come properly equipped they could not cook at this time. On the next meeting day everyone remembered her equipment.

Letting the girls, in free discussion, agree on what is necessary to do the job generally solves the problem much more effectively than if the teacher arbitrarily decides what needs to be done. Once the girls have agreed, it is far less likely that a student will transgress.

THE USE OF GRADES

The use of grades as a consequence has often been suggested. However, grades can rarely be considered as a consequence; they are more likely to be considered either a reward for effort or ability or punishment for the lack of the same. In the following example, however, a grade appeared to have the effect of a logical consequence.

Example 93

Monty was an excellent athlete. He entered high school with the desire to attend college on an athletic scholarship. He had been a very good student during his freshman year. But when he was in his sophomore year the glory of his athletic prowess was more than he could accept without noticeable change in his behavior. He began to disregard important assignments. Monty and I had always been friends; while I was chatting with him one day, I asked him if he wanted to see the number of assignments he had failed to hand in. He said that he did, and I explained that sometimes these were very important and could affect his nine weeks' grade. He seemed surprised that he had submitted so few papers, but continued to do little about it. When the end of the grading period came, Monty received a failing grade, seemingly much to his surprise; he said nothing, but was obviously disturbed. The following day he asked if he could talk with me and I said that I would see him. During my free period I called him in and he told me that he appreciated my giving him a flunking grade. He realized that it was essential that one not overlook his responsibilities in his academic work more than any of his responsibilities to the team. He went so far as to say that this was the most important instance in his training and that it would definitely influence his reaction and conformity to situations that he would experience in the future.

Generally a failing grade is punishment and perceived as such. In our example Monty had been a good student but had decided to let the glory of his athletic achievements carry him. Often teachers are unwilling or have pressure put upon them not to fail students who are outstanding members of athletic teams. In this case Monty received ample warning, in a nonthreatening way; when he still failed to fulfill his assignments he was given the failing grade. Perhaps because he had not expected this to happen, and because he had gotten by before, the shock was enough to make him realize that he could no longer get away with avoiding his responsibilities.

NEGLECTING RESPONSIBILITY

Often becoming a star or leader in athletic performances leads a student to tend to neglect his other responsibilities; this might not occur were there less glory attached to athletic achievements. Dealing with such a situation often will set an example that discourages further neglect, such as the following case indicates:

Example 94

Last year I was the baseball coach at my school. I was for-
tunate enough to inherit an exceptionally fine team from my
predecessor. He was also good enough to inform me that
in addition to the potential championship caliber, the group
also had an overabundance of prima donnas. There seemed
to be a reluctance on the part of a few individuals to show
up for practice each night. The former coach treated the
infraction of training by making the violators run extra
laps around the field when they returned to practice. He
invited me to do the same. I did carry on with the procedure with varying success until the final weeks of the
season. Then I dropped a real bomb. I announced that
anyone missing practice would not play in the final game,
which, incidentally, might have meant the championship.
Trying me out, I assume, my shortstop and catcher, both
very important cogs in my team setup, missed the last
practice prior to our last game. True to my word, I held
them both out of the game, in the face of much grumbling,
parental pressures, and many insinuations. My vindication
came when their replacements, who had not had much
opportunity to play all year, were both instrumental in our
victory and championship.

One might wonder what would have happened if the
team had not won the championship. At the same time, this
teacher is to be commended for his courage in sticking to
his decision; however, it would have been better had he
been less arbitrary and had called upon the team for a decision. Then he might have taken less risk even if the team
had not won.

Example 95

The track team of a small private high school was returnmg
by chartered bus from the track meet. A number of the boys

in the bus began to pelt passing automobiles with oranges
that had been furnished for their refreshment. One of the
automobiles happened to be driven by an off-duty policeman. The policeman stopped the bus and obtained information about the school. The next morning the principal received a citation fining the school five hundred dollars for
responsibility for this act. The principal called all the boys
into a special assembly. The circumstances of the incident
were presented along with the fine of five hundred dollars.
The boys were asked if any of those responsible wanted to
stand and accept responsibility for the act and assume
responsibility for the payment of the fine. None volun-
teered. The principal then said that the fine was to be
paid and the only source of money was to be from the next
year's athletic fund. This was for one year for all sports
and amounted to only seven hundred and fifty dollars. All
athletic events for that year would have to be eliminated
for the lack of funds. The thought of the school losing all
athletic events for one year was a more personal loss to
the boys than having their parents pay the fine, which would
have happened had they originally admitted their guilt or
had the whole team been fined. The boys felt so guilty
about the incident they held a meeting to determine how
they could remove the shame as well as the fine. They
wrote a letter of apology to the police officer for the incident, explaining to him how they felt about involving the
rest of the school. The letter must have been convincing.
The officer took it to the proper authorities and was instrumental in having the fine reduced to fifty dollars. This was
paid for out of the track team portion of the athletic fund.

Perhaps the most important factor was that when the
members of the track team saw that the whole athletic program of the school would be imperiled, they were forced
into assuming responsibility. In this case other members of
the team probably could have stopped the transgressors in
time if they had realized that they would have to share the

responsibility. It is important for those not directly involved in misdemeanors to realize that they can be held accountable as well, being members of the group, particularly if they are in a position to do something about stopping the misbehaviors.

THE ROLL CALL

Example 96

As a student teacher I am vulnerable to the whims of the students when I take over the class, and I am tried out in many instances. I can remember once walking into a class of high school seniors, new in the school. The regular teacher had left her roll book so I might take roll, but no seating chart. So, I called the role and the students answered. I could see smiles on four boys' faces. I suspected that these boys were answering for each other, and I made a mental note to each answer. During the class the students were being graded on their oral ability to answer questions. I called on one boy with the name to which he had answered. He did not know the answer, so I put a zero in the book for the name. Then an immediate protest was heard from the "real" boy. The grade was kept in the book, and when I returned the next day all of the students answered correctly to the roll call.

Being a substitute teacher, particularly at the high school level, demands quickness in sizing up the situation and ingenuity in keeping ahead of the "testers." Unfortunately, few adults, parents and teachers alike, are a match for the resourceful children.

TAKING EXAMS

Example 97

Taking exams is always a challenge to the students and to the teacher who wants order. The students are told in this particular classroom that there is to be no talking during an exam as others want to think and it is not a time one likes to be disturbed. Anyone talking and disturbing his fellow classmates will have his exam removed. He will be given the choice of taking half of the grade obtained in the time spent on the exam or coming in after school and taking a new exam. Thus, the student always has the chance to make up the work, but suffers the consequence of finding the work more inconvenient.

Though this seems to be a rather ingenious procedure, again letting the group participate in finding a solution to the disruption would have been preferable. The teacher could perhaps during the discussion suggest the particular method, and if the students then agreed upon it, there would be more likelihood of cooperation.

DEFACING SCHOOL PROPERTY

Example 98

One day during a drafting class I discovered a student scratching his initials in the wooden blade of a T square issued to him at the beginning of the semester. The students were made aware of their responsibility to care for and maintain the drawing instruments, as accuracy is so necessary to a good drawing. The student was presented with the choice of paying for the T square, two dollars and a half, since he had his initials on it and could take it home, or trying to restore it to the original state in which it was issued to him. He decided to try to restore it. "Two-fifty is a lot of money for this thing," he replied. He was sent to the workshop with the T square where he had to sandpaper the initials off the blade. To completely restore the instrument it was necessary for the whole blade to be sanded. After sanding, it had to be lacquered and allowed to dry overnight. The next day, before the class, he brought in the T square and handed it to me satisfactorily refinished.

Here again is an example where the teacher could have been a great deal more effective if rules regarding equipment had been discussed by the group and the decision made that this would be the choice of anyone who had defaced the equipment. In the following instance, the decision, if arbitrarily imposed by the school authorities, probably would have broken down, but because the students were involved in the decision-making process the consequence was effective.

Example 99

The incident under discussion has to do with a messy unkempt school ground at the junior high school where I teach. A suggestion was made by the student council, and approved by the principal, that if the student body chose not to pick up their food and paper scraps following their lunch period and before going to the next class, the custodian would hoist up a black flag (the flagpole was erected in the center of their lunch area behind the school, so as not to confuse the public, where it would be a reminder for all). This signified that there would be no nutrition break the next day, instead regular classwork. Since the teachers also missed their nutrition break, they made sure the student body had plenty of work to do. Some days a few students would pick up the scraps for the whole group. Some days most of them pitched in and cleaned up the yard, and on other days the effort was not enough to pass inspection. My first thought was that the black flag was not a logical consequence; but I think what is signified is that each day the students had to make a choice whether they wanted a nutrition break the following day. As a result, the custodians had three hours more each day to do work which was more constructive and it gave the students a sense of pride in their school.

In this case the decision made was in the nature of a punishment. It was effective because it had been decided on by a duly elected council composed of members of the students' choice. Often students are as punitive as adults, or even more so. What made the decision a part of a logical consequence was the fact that the teachers, too, were deprived of their nutrition break. This made the procedure one of "distributive justice" (Piaget)

MARKING UP THE SCHOOL WALLS

Example 100

The two fourteen-year-old girls were laughingly walking all around the Sunday-school building marking "X's" and "hi's" and drawing little faces with chalk all over the doors, steps, floors, walls, and elsewhere. Bible school had just been dismissed for the day and all the other children had already gone home. Only a teacher straightening things up was there. Though she knew what they were doing, she did not pay any attention to them in spite of the noise they were making to get her attention. Instead, she waited until they were making their last few marks on the steps leading to the outside and then she asked them if they did not now realize that they would have to clean it all up. She gave them rags and buckets of water to clean up all the marks they had made.

A question might be raised as to why the teacher allowed the girls to go ahead and mark up the walls, even though she was aware of their misbehavior. Stopping them would be just exactly what the girls expected; therefore the teacher showed wisdom and foresight in allowing them to go ahead until they had covered such an area that it would take a considerable time for them to clean the mess up. In this case the teacher did not allow herself to fall for what might have been the usual response.

GROUP CONSEQUENCES

As discussed in regard to elementary school students, logical group consequences can also be effective in high schools.

Example 101

My Russian class was small, consisting of only eight eleventh- and twelfth-graders. One day as I entered the classroom and as soon as I began taking papers from my briefcase the students engaged in conversation completely ignoring my presence. Fortunately, I managed to control my first impulse to call them to order and acted as though nothing were happening. I started working on homeroom papers of another class. I must admit, that it seemed to me the students would continue indefinitely. Finally, to my relief, I noticed that they were signaling to each other and a certain quietness filled the classroom. I continued to put on an act for a short interval, trying to make every second count. Then I quietly collected my papers, looked at the class and said, "Thank you, I suppose we may proceed with the lesson."

It is interesting to note, though the teacher was impatient and annoyed, he still managed to stick to his plan and soon the situation was in order. Instead of talking he acted, and let the situation exert its influence.

Example 102

My ninth-grade art class was given the opportunity to choose cooperatively from several projects that interested them. Then they were to divide into small interest groups to complete their project. I explained to the class that the choice should be made that day and they could begin work immediately. Bedlam broke loose. All students began talking at once and did not stop as they usually did when I stopped and waited for quiet. I went to the blackboard, and began to write up a one-day sketching assignment. By the time I had finished writing, the room was quiet. I said we would do this assignment today. If they felt ready to do some group planning tomorrow then we could continue. The class went right to work on the assignment and the next day we had one of the best cooperative planning sessions we ever had.

In this case the teacher wisely ignored the bedlam and went into action. Since their behavior indicated that they were not ready to do planning for the group project that day, it would have to be deferred until the following day. The students got the allusion without words and responded accordingly.

Example 103

Students in my mathematics class had a tendency to be noisy after the bell had rung which meant it was time to start class. At first I used to ask them several times to be quiet. I would say, "The bell has rung." I am sure, though, that they had all heard it. After this method did not work, I just sat there and didn't say a thing, but waited for them to get quiet. And when the bell rang for lunch, I did not excuse them, but went right on with the lesson and excused them about three minutes later. That was how long it had taken them to settle down. The next day they settled down thirty seconds after the bell rang, so we stayed thirty seconds after the bell had rung for lunch. The third day, when the bell rang to start class they were quiet; and from then on they were quiet when it was time to begin.

In this example time was brought in as an element of social order. Perhaps the most interesting and important aspect of this example was that the teacher made no attempt to explain why she was holding them, or even to indicate the length of time they had spent at the beginning before quieting down. The students quickly realized what her intent was; and as soon as they understood this, they were ready to go to work immediately and without undue consideration.

Epilogue

Let us consider what benefit the reader may have received from this volume. The presentation of a definite technique cannot immediately make the reader an expert in its application. Underlying what appears to be merely a technical procedure is a definite philosophy. Both the acquisition of a skill in using a technique and reorienting one's thoughts and values require time.

This book, like all others which describe our methods, is intended to serve as a guide. It requires careful study and reflection to grasp its full meaning, to recognize the fine difference between traditional methods and those presented here.

Parents and teachers do not abdicate their function as educators; they merely redefine their role as leaders of their wards. While we concern ourselves with more effective ways of influencing our children and youth, we are establishing a new form of personal relationships, appropriate for living as equals in a democracy.

INDEX

Index